COSMIC VEDIC TECHNOLOGY

PROFESSOR SANJAY ROUT

The Book Is Dedicated To All My Friends, Family, Parents And Almighty. Special Thanks To All the Reviewers, Designers and Technical Teams. For Whom This Entire Book Can Be Possible.

ꕥ

Contents

Foreword

Preface

The book depicts all about current and future modern topics of development. This is an approach and perception of transformation in development. The book is for all cater to the audience throughout the globe.

ACKNOWLEDGEMENTS

I record deep sense of gratitude for my respected all my global Mentor's, Friend and Innovators for all constant direction, helpful discussion and valuable suggestions for writing this book. Due to his valuable suggestions and regular encouragement. I would be able to complete this work and fulfillment of my dream. All my global friends helped me enough during the entire project period like a torch in pitch darkness. I shall remain highly indebted to all throughout my life. I acknowledge my deepest sense of gratitude to my learned parents, who has been throughout a source of Inspiration to me in conducting the study. Who helped me at various stages of the study directly or indirectly. He also enlightened me to follow the path of duty. Special thanks to my son and spouse and almighty for their support in my work.

Prologue

The book is written by Professor Sanjay Rout and Edited by Professor Prangyan Biswal , Published by ISL Publications. The book is available in all leading global stores. This book depicts future transformation thoughts of developments.

Secret Yogic Techniques

The most amazing technique to connect superior cosmic energy is yoga. The yogic technique Yam-rules are extraordinary. Maharishi Patanjali has said in its Yogic philosophy that important Riddhi Siddhisi receives important from the sadhana of these ten.Our privilege is that the spirit of the soul is a true development of the soul and due to which life becomes full of happiness and peace.

The implementation of Yama-Rule is similar to the moving on a highway that leaves directly to the destination site. 'Highway' means common-road-on which everyone can walk, on which everything is simplicity, facility, no special difficulty is not in front.

It is similar to Rajas. The Yogic's sadhana can do everybody, it can progress in it and succeed, it is a Raja. Hathoga, Kundalini Yogic, rhythm, oasis, etc. is not as simple and their right is to every man.

There is special preparations for them, and there is a special type of tolerance, but there are no such conditions in Rajas, because they are for a man, women and women, child-aged, educated for everyone. Equally useful and simple.

Yogic means to meet. The sadhana can meet the divine of the soul, it is called Yogic.

The biggest success of the creature is to get God, to become a little bigger, to be completed from the incomplete, to be free from the bond, it is trying to try the past, crossing the thunder It has been increased so much, that journey is to meet God, it is looking for his sweetness mother, it is snatched to sít ín the dock. The sadhana of that late mílítant ís the name of the same, straíghtforward, símple, whích ís the name of the name.

Maharíshí Patanjalí has dívíded thís Yogíc ínto eíght parts. 29th formula of footprínt two ís

Yama Rehabílítatíon Pranayama Agreement

Perceptíon Medítatíon Samadhanganí

Thís ís eíght parts of yam, rules, posture, pranayama, antíst perceptíon and samadhí Yogíc.

Footer of Yogíc-phílosophy has been told ín relatíon to Yama ín 30- Ahímsa Satyestay Brahmírpírrahaha Yama. That ís, non-víolence, truth, outrage, brahmacharya and unrestrícted are fíve yams.

Readers should not be confused wíth the word Yama, the god of death ís also called Yama, here there ís no ímplementatíon here. Here ít has been named after a noun of the above fíve verses. From the word Yama here ís the only príce of fíve verses. A further explanatíon ís done respectívely.,

Ashtang Yogíc, the fírst límb - Yama

Yamas

Yamas

Fíve Yama descríbed ín Yogsutra by Maharíshí Patanjalí

Non víolence

truth

Aastay

Brahmacharya

Unnecessary

Ten Yama descríbed by Shandyyya Upaníshad and Swatmaram-

- Non víolence
- truth
- Aastay
- Brahmacharya
- Forgíveness
- Duct
- Mercy
- Argav
- Míthar
- Defecatíon

Non violence

Non-violence is called non-violence. Nonviolence means killing, sadness. The meaning is free. Thus, non-violence has happened, do not kill, do not grieve. These tasks are called violence by whom someone reaches physical or mental suffering, so they are unhappy for the person who followed the fasting.,

According to Mahatma Gandhi-quietness is only violence, excitement is violence, misery is violence, hatred is violence, anyone's violence is violence, whose world needs to be captured, it is also violence, to kill someone, to kill someone If the heart is sad, it is a violence, it will be said to be the most important non-violence.,

In general, non-violence in the above rows, it is incomplete and incomprehensible factor. If a person remained far away from the contact of people and sitting in the sitting-sitting food, we could not even follow such non-violence to any extent, because many creatures will die in breathing, In keeping the water, the micro-burning will be killed, in keeping the feet, there will be a few creatures in laying, keeping the body and clothing net, they will die, sometimes in the stomach, they will die..

Even if there is a certain avoidance from gross violence, that solitary service can not follow the whole nonviolence. What to do? Do not kill self? Or is it disappointed by climbing the first ladder of Yogic path?

Only the sense of non-violence can not be found, for this, Yogiraj Krishna will have to take charge of practical education given to Arjun. Arjuna sees that in the war there will be such an immense army, so many humans will be killed, it is a violence, it will take a heavy pity, he keeps the bow in the last part of the chariot and says that, O Achyut! I will not make such a big sin for a few state greed, I will not be trend in this war.,

Lord Krishna resolved Yogic in eighteen chapters of Geeta while resolving this doubt of Arjuna, he explained to many arguments, evidence, principles and perspectives that do not give suffocations of non-violence, wicked, mischief It is also non-violence to kill, unrecognized, atrocities, sinful and pajis.

The violence that the non-violence was born, the fight which is found in peace, there is nothing inappropriate or unarmed in it.

Krishna said to Arjuna, leaving this thick wisdom and considering a subtle, there is no prestige of non-violence that it is less difficult to suffer, it is not a matter of particular importance, because the body is always It is only destroyed and the soul is immortal, so there is no violence in killing. Nonviolence means to be hatred,

Inspired by the private rage hatred, the work that is done without considering the world's interest. If for public welfare, there is no blame in anybody who has to kill anyone for the increase of religion.

Arjun made a good way of God's words and when he understood the realization of non-violence, the Mahabharata had gathered. Even after the eighteen axis army, Arjun did not feel anything sin.

There is an affair promise that there is no violence of Vedic violence, violence. In the greed of Ziwa's cleverness, there is a knife to knock on their neck to eat the flesh and useful animal-birds.

For the sadhana of its inappropriate selfishness, there is violence to sorrow innocent people. But if he is suffering for public welfare and for the beneficiary of the same creature, he would not have violence but will be non-violence.

Doctor with a selflessness of the patient's actual service, a justified judge orders the death penalty for the arrangement of the robber to maintain society. A religious publicity is the path of penance for self-welfare. Moves in.

It looks like a thick vision, it seems like all violence but in fact it is true nonviolence. The abundant seems to be a non-violent in seeing the miscreants, who donate wickedness, donating wickedness, is a terrible pity, violent, killer.,

He unknowingly becomes helpful in producing the poisonous belt of wickedness to produce deadly fruits for the world, such non-violence can call the non-violence of the ignorant.

Patanjali Yogic Darshan is said in the 2-formula 35. It has been said that inhalation of non-violence. Bizarre, hatred, vengeance of anyone's mind or to suffer the body is absolutely unfair, should avoid caution from this violence.

Non violence means the priest of love, devoid of malice. If you need to suffer from goodwill and discretion wisdom, then there is a scope under the limit of non-violence. The non-violent has to leave the hatred, it has to be overcome, there is a lot to get rid of a private loss, generous, fair and justified, then it will be decided by that approach. .

Violence for Paramarth cannot be held less than any kind of non-violence.

Mahatma Gandhi's statement is that from non-violence, we learn to make a friend, the glory of God's truth is more and more life, peace and happiness also increases, our courage increases. We learn the idea of duty.

Pride is away, humility increases. The harvest is less comfortable and the filled scum in the body becomes less. Non-violence is not the religion of heroes. By sacrificing hats, love emotion, intimacy, giving a prominent place, to combat evil is non-violence.,

To increase bravery, boldness, clarity, integrity, to the extent that the arrow sword is trivial in front of it, the sadhana of non-violence. Uncondition is not distracted when understanding the body's mortality, there is no opportunity to stay.

The vision of non-violent is to give pleasure to others, removal of iniquity and ignorance can be achieved by sadness and happiness. The priest of non-violence does the strongest effort to remove the unrighteous and ignorance of the other, which has achieved true and permanent pleasure, for this great work, if your or others have to endure some pain, then it is appropriate. It always remains ready.

Truth

It is said that the thing is similar to the same thing. But this definition of truth is very incomplete and incincent.,

Truth is a very wide and comprehensive element. He is the head of all in the base pillars of creation. True Speech is a very small molecule of that great truth, as much as possible, a drop of water in comparison to the sea.

It should be true, but before speaking the truth, the prevalence of truth and its element should be killed, because it has to be broken or in the ornamental language, because the distinction between the country, time and the character. In the religious texts, the fruits of rituals have been written very much.

Like to destroy the sin of seven births from the Ganga bath, the fasting, making heaven from fasting, go to the donation, to get rid of idol worship, all these things are unrealized by knowledge, because the purity in mind with these committees It is understandable, but it does not understand that it does not understand that what is the need for great means like great fruits such as minor actions? Tech Sier's market remains hot,

Now the question is present whether the religion is a false false? Did the creators of those teams have made unreal speech? Not even in his statement, there is no lie across and he has done unreal speech from any self-interest.,

He explained in a particular way in a special way, examining his psychiatils to a special category, truthfulness, unconsciousness, lazy and greedy persons. It was necessary for the individuals of such a category, so that order of religious texts is true in a range.

While stripping the ointment on the baby boils, the doctor gives him comfort. Children! Do not be afraid, there will be no problem. The child believes in his point, but the doctor's talk comes out.

Children have a lot of trouble at the time of the ointment strip, he thinks that the doctor is false, he did unreal speech with me, but in reality he does not lie.

Teacher teaches lessons to children, teach mathematics, to give them such examples, which are unrealistic and unreal, yet the teacher is not called false.

Those who become mental diseases or becomes vigilant to become a ghost, their tantric or psychological treatment has to be done in such a way that the victim will get out. When the ghost looks good, it is good, if the Baham is told, then the patient will not fill the mind and his suffering will not eradicate.

In the treatment of tantric and psychology, the patient has to do good by lying, but he is not held in the category of all lies.

Many times a lie is proved to be true in politics. Can be lied to defend yourself from the wicked. The couple does not reveal their secret. Economic business or other similar distinctions are not often told.,

Sometimes speaking truth is also prohibited. Saying Kana and Langada to Langada, there is a truth speech. The military is considered to be a criminal to reveal the secret or the enemy's true notice of his country and he gets harsh punishment from the law. What is the true speech to tell the butcher of the Bhagged Cow?

Thus, it is a very big illusion to make the truth in speaking, in which the unbelievable person can be confused. The truth is that taking care of the country, time and character for public welfare, it has to be taken from the unnecessary truth speech. The word from which others are good, encouragement for the culture, it is true.

Many times, on the false praise of the inferior characters, they are divided into a type of public and according to hypnosis, they are really praised to be appreciable.

Such untrue speech will be called truth. If it is opened by opening a person's flaws, it becomes the same as it is disappointed, defeated and degenerated. Such truth ís also íncreased by false.

The defínítíon of speech should be the defínítíon of the truth that there ís a lot of ínterest and ít ís unreal. The Ramayana preached that the pregnancy of fríendshíp ís revealed that Dura ís consídered to be untrue, relígíon.

How truth ís your speech, how much false, on thís críteríon, how much ínterest and how much harm ís ít? There ís advancement of goodwíll or decadence, the development of socíetíes or destructíon.,

Wíth the sacred purpose, ít ís unrealístíc, ít ís unrealístíc for charíty, and wíth bad íntentíons, the truth ís also untrue. Thís marm should be banned ín Gírah.

The actual and comprehensíve truth ís a hígh object. He ís not a speech, but ít ís a matter of recognízíng. All the poets are ínterpreted accordíng to theír vísíon of the same great element. What ís the purpose and actíon of what ís the purpose and work-cause, what ís the purpose and work due to the dancer, what ís the dancer, what ís the purpose and work reason. Ít ís researchíng truth.

II

By getting information about God, the creature, nature, it is a pole of human life to move forward to get the ultimate post by removing its illusions. Our continued industry should be to achieve the same truth.

Lord Ved Vyas has given the consolation of truth while speaking of 2/38 -

Paratar Savabodh Satrante Bagupta Like If Vinnowda Bharanda and Opening Bandy and Bhawaditi Ath Savrataparkarthar Tips, If the Chaiyamabhimana Ghatopatha Purvasanya Satyan Bhavit Papamava Bhavit

That is, the truth is whether it is cheated, illusion, anticipation, or free. So be used by the persecution of the living and not for the undesirable of a creature. If there is a truth, it is harmed to the creatures - then it is not true.,

It is only true Satyan and such truth is transformed into untruth and becomes a sin factor. Like the butcher asked that the cow has gone here? If yes it is answered then it is not true even if it seems to be truth, the effective creature is fatal. If there is no other remedy, it is also true to make unreal speech for discretion.

Mahabharata has given the message of truth -

Neither the element is true, neither the element involvement.

If the best interests are correct.

It is not true to say that it is not true to say that it is unreal. There is more interest in the fact that the same is true.

To make the truth an adjective of the speech, it is to humiliate that creation. Speaking is a minor thing in which it can be done as needed. To find the truth, find out the reality and whatever it seems true, it is hard to persist, it is true.

The second ladder of Yama does not speak truth, it is to be true. It should be done with courage, boldness and honesty to be truthful than being truthful of the practítioner of Yogíc path.

Aastay

Do not steal, thís ís the bríef meaníng, the purí ís called theft to take the secretly wíthout hís command. Ínappropríate kídnappíng of the second earníngs ís stolen, on the matter whích ís not self índependence, ít ís necessary to take ít ín the ínformatíon or rapíng ít, ít wíll be saíd, "Ít ís saíd.

Takíng a certaín thíng wíthout íts acceptance ís the fat meaníng of theft. Anímal mílk, sheep haír, honey of flíes, ít ís also a sake thíng and are also taken wíthout acceptance. Father's earníng property ís a sake, even íf the father does not want, he wíll get the son's ríght to the son.,

The court recovers the penalty, the candídor recovers íncome tax, chaggí etc., he ís afraíd and the owner does not even gíve ít even íf he ís not stealíng. (1) Paraí cheese and (2) wíthout obedíence can not be a fíne decísíon on the condítíon of these two elements. Suppose that the person ís prepared to gíve an object due to pressure

And he commands ín helplessness, díd he become unhealthy? A person has deposíted hís second to the other, but now the ídea tells hís own coalísm on hím and refuses to return the real owner, whether he should not return to hím.

Ís there any reason to get the ríght thíng ín the present tíme and should not leave that balance due to non-commandment?

There can be a lot of confusíon on the obstacle of the fat and excessíve. Many tímes ít happens that even íf the object does not have any questíons, ít does not even raíse the questíon. Even then ít becomes stolen. Just líke a shopkeeper keeps íts sharpness, passíng passage ín the fleece or there ís no need to order anybody to get ríd of them or to take so much of them.

Ín the place of Síer (1 Síer = 933 Víllage), he gave fífteen cheetock (1 cheeted = 58 grams), he was saved, accordíng to the líteral defínítíon, he díd not really get ínto theft. Ís . Taílor saves cloth ín sewíng, draggíng the dhobí clothíng several days, save the míll flour, the servant bríngs seven pases on the money of eíght money, the real owner can not fínd these thíeves,

Even íf ít does not even get more attentíon, then the calculatíon wíll not be ín theft, the owner does not know hís loss and contínue to do somethíng secretly or índírectly, even íf he could not be revealed.

Theft of duty ís a great stolen of íts kínd. Sometímes ít has been stopped by decídíng the wages and to work ín ít, lazíness, whích ís stolen, nowadays, ít ís the same thíng as ít ís theft, líke breakíng someone's lock.

Responding to the responsibility of doing reliable secret tasks, revealing its distinction, making someone's masterpiece, it is stolen. Do not pay your duty, neglecting dependents, enjoy themselves special features, it also comes in the same limit, such as hiding with children. If you get a lying thing, your master should reach it, should be revealed at all or the owner does not know if the officer should be handed over.

If this is not done and the object is quietly kept quiet, then it is also stolen, for not working, for the incidental item, it is the task of this category.

Taking a prize in return for their due duty, taking a gift to the notable work, these two types of bribes are theft. What kind of bribe is hot, it is not hidden from anyone, which has been fixed for the work, asks its right to do the same thing, bribe has started to be called.

It is not necessary for any special grace, but it is necessary to fulfill the work from the well-being, if not given, such obstacles are inserted. Those who are tough to be bigger for a middle-term man. On giving more rights, they do not laugh at laughter.

From the people who should be expected of justice and Somewhat, the bribe has taken the form of rights, theft has become sinjora. These actions should be closed now.

The real meaning is to mean that your actual rights should be taken comfortably by theft, it can be easily ridiculed by theft, which should be taken by the fact that the amount of money should be given to themselves.

Think about what you are getting, what exactly is my religion on this matter? I am not eating any other part? Am more I should get more than that? Is not you lacking your duty? Those who should not give them without giving them? If your received object is tightened on these five questions, then it may seem that there is no stolen or how much it is the stolen.

Someone is stolen by breaking the lock or cut the pocket, as well as keep error in duty and taking more than the right. Avoiding these thieves, depending on their sweat earnings.

It is necessary to protect themselves from theft, and others should also save, at least to cooperate in theft. If there is a loss by giving a bribe, then that loss should be tolerated, because in the murder of animal, the sellers, eating, everyone cooks seem to be sin in the work of theft. By giving help to help or increase the courage of theft, it has to be part of sin.

If someone or someone else kidnapped any wicked mischief, then there should be struggle against it so that there is a small amount of stolen and ignorant in the world family. Do not steal yourself and do not let others have two parts of the same religion, the seeker of the Yogic route should keep in mind the same way, like the bicycle rotates equally.

The actual and comprehensive truth is a high object. He is not a speech, but it is a matter of recognizing. All the poets are interpreted according to their vision of the same great element. What is the purpose and action of what is the purpose and work-cause, what is the purpose and work due to the dancer, what is the dancer, what is the purpose and work reason. It is researching truth. By getting information about God, the creature, nature, it is a pole of human life to move forward to get the ultimate post by removing its illusions. Our continued industry should be to achieve the same truth.

Lord Ved Vyas has given the consolation of truth while speaking of 2/38 -

Paratar Savabodh Satrante Bagupta Like If Vinnowda Bharanda and Opening Bandy and Bhawaditi

Ath Savrataparkarthar Tips, If the Chaiyamabhimana Ghatopatha Purvasanya Satyan Bhavit Papamava Bhavit

That is, the truth is whether it is cheated, illusion, anticipation, or free. So be used by the persecution of the living and not for the undesirable of a creature. If there is a truth, it is harmed to the creatures - then it is not true.,

It is only true Satyan and such truth is transformed into untruth and becomes a sin factor. Like the butcher asked that the cow has gone here? If yes it is answered then it is not true even if it seems to be truth, the effective creature is fatal. If there is no other remedy, it is also true to make unreal speech for discretion.

Mahabharata has given the message of truth -

Neither the element is true, neither the element involvement.

If the best interests are correct.

It is not true to say that it is not true to say that it is unreal. There is more interest in the fact that the same is true.

To make the truth an adjective of the speech, it is to humiliate that creation. Speaking is a minor thing in which it can be done as needed. To find the truth, find out the reality and whatever it seems true, it is hard to persist, it is true.

The second ladder of Yama does not speak truth, it is to be true. It should be done with courage, boldness and honesty to be truthful than being truthful of the practitioner of Yogic path.

Aastay

Do not steal, this is the brief meaning, the puri is called theft to take the secretly without his command. Inappropriate kidnapping of the second earnings is stolen, on the matter which is not self independence, it is necessary to take it in the information or raping it, it will be said, "It is said.

Taking a certain thing without its acceptance is the fat meaning of theft. Animal milk, sheep hair, honey of flies, it is also a sake thing and are also taken without acceptance. Father's earning property is a sake, even if the father does not want, he will get the son's right to the son.,

The court recovers the penalty, the candidor recovers income tax, chaggi etc., he is afraid and the owner does not even give it even if he is not stealing. (1) Parai cheese and (2) without obedience can not be a fine decision on the condition of these two elements. Suppose that the person is prepared to give an object due to pressure

And he commands in helplessness, did he become unhealthy? A person has deposited his second to the other, but now the idea tells his own coalism on him and refuses to return the real owner, whether he should not return to him.

Is there any reason to get the right thing in the present time and should not leave that balance due to non-commandment?

There can be a lot of confusion on the obstacle of the fat and excessive.

Many times it happens that even if the object does not have any questions, it does not even raise the question. Even then it becomes stolen. Just like a shopkeeper keeps its sharpness, passing passage in the fleece or there is no need to order anybody to get rid of them or to take so much of them.

In the place of Sier (1 Sier = 933 Village), he gave fifteen cheetock (1 cheeted = 58 grams), he was saved, according to the literal definition, he did not really get into theft. Is . Tailor saves cloth in sewing, dragging the dhobi clothing several days, save the mill flour, the servant brings seven pases on the money of eight money, the real owner can not find these thieves,

Even if it does not even get more attention, then the calculation will not be in theft, the owner does not know his loss and continue to do something secretly or indirectly, even if he could not be revealed.

Theft of duty is a great stolen of its kind. Sometimes it has been stopped by deciding the wages and to work in it, laziness, which is stolen, nowadays, it is the same thing as it is theft, like breaking someone's lock.

Responding to the responsibility of doing reliable secret tasks, revealing its distinction, making someone's masterpiece, it is stolen. Do not pay your duty, neglecting dependents, enjoy themselves special features, it also comes in the same limit, such as hiding with children. If you get a lying thing, your master should reach it, should be revealed at all or the owner does not know if the officer should be handed over.

If this is not done and the object is quietly kept quiet, then it is also stolen, for not working, for the incidental item, it is the task of this category.

Taking a prize in return for their due duty, taking a gift to the notable work, these two types of bribes are theft. What kind of bribe is hot, it is not hidden from anyone, which has been fixed for the work, asks its right to do the same thing, bribe has started to be called.

It is not necessary for any special grace, but it is necessary to fulfill the work from the well-being, if not given, such obstacles are inserted. Those who are tough to be bigger for a middle-term man. On giving more rights, they do not laugh at laughter.

From the people who should be expected of justice and Somewhat, the bribe has taken the form of rights, theft has become sinjora. These actions should be closed now.

The real meaning is to mean that your actual rights should be taken comfortably by theft, it can be easily ridiculed by theft, which should be taken by the fact that the amount of money should be given to themselves.

Think about what you are getting, what exactly is my religion on this matter? I am not eating any other part? Am more I should get more than that? Is not you lacking your duty? Those who should not give them without giving them? If your received object is tightened on these five questions, then it may seem that there is no stolen or how much it is the stolen.

Someone is stolen by breaking the lock or cut the pocket, as well as keep error in duty and taking more than the right. Avoiding these thieves, depending on their sweat earnings.

It is necessary to protect themselves from theft, and others should also save, at least to cooperate in theft. If there is a loss by giving a bribe, then that loss should be tolerated, because in the murder of animal, the sellers, eating, everyone cooks seem to be sin in the work of theft. By giving help to help or increase the courage of theft, it has to be part of sin.

If someone or someone else kidnapped any wicked mischief, then there should be struggle against it so that there is a small amount of stolen and ignorant in the world family. Do not steal yourself and do not let others have two parts of the same religion, the seeker of the Yogic route should keep in mind the same way, like the bicycle rotates equally.

The actual and comprehensive truth is a high object. He is not a speech, but it is a matter of recognizing. All the poets are interpreted according to their vision of the same great element. What is the purpose and action of what is the purpose and work-cause, what is the purpose and work due to the dancer, what is the dancer, what is the purpose and work reason. It is researching truth. By getting information about God, the creature, nature, it is a pole of human life to move forward to get the ultimate post by removing its illusions. Our continued industry should be to achieve the same truth.

Lord Ved Vyas has given the consolation of truth while speaking of 2/38 -

Paratar Savabodh Satrante Bagupta Like If Vinnowda Bharanda and Opening Bandy and Bhawaditi Ath Savrataparkarthar Tips, If the Chaiyamabhimana Ghatopatha Purvasanya Satyan Bhavit Papamava Bhavit

That is, the truth is whether it is cheated, illusion, anticipation, or free. So be used by the persecution of the living and not for the undesirable of a creature. If there is a truth about the realistic things, then it is not true.

It is only true Satyan and such truth is transformed into untruth and becomes a sin factor. Like the butcher asked that the cow has gone here? If yes it is answered then it is not true even if it seems to be truth, the effective creature is fatal. If there is no other remedy, it is also true to make unreal speech for discretion.

Mahabharata has given the message of truth -

Neither the element is true, neither the element involvement.

If the best interests are correct.

It is not true to say that it is not true to say that it is unreal. There is more interest in the fact that the same is true.

To make the truth an adjective of the speech, it is to humiliate that creation. Speaking is a minor thing in which it can be done as needed. Finding the truth, finding the reality and whatever it seems true, it is hard to persist, it is true. The second ladder of Yama does not speak the truth, the truth is to be done.,

It should be done with courage, boldness and honesty to be truthful than being truthful of the practitioner of Yogic path.

Brahmacharya

Generally, the meaning of Brahmacharya does not understand the semen. The person who avoids a woman contact is called Brahmachari. This half meaning, half is still remaining.,

Brahma means to conduct life in God, to get tiredness, in the research of truth, removing the mind and the conduct of Brahma. There is also one to do not do it in its means.

Mahatma Gandhi has said a very best in this regard - remember the original meaning of the Brahmacharya. In the research of Brahmacharya, the truth of the truth, the Ethics,

From this basic sense, the special meaning of surveyed restraint is just forgotten the incomplete meaning of public restraint. The genital detention has been considered to be followed by Brahmacharya. In my opinion, it is incomplete and false interpretation.

The disclosure of the subject is only Brahmacharya. Those who try to stop only one Indree by going to the senses where they wandered here, he tries sterilize. Listening to the things of the disorder, seeing the eye disorder, tasting the behavioral object from the tongue, touching the things that penetrate the disorders by hand and to prevent the masses, add it to the fire and avoid burning. The similarity was to try.

That is why the person who decides to stop the genitals should be taken by the initiative to stop the effort to stop the disorders of the senses.

I have always experienced that the compressed interpretation of the Brahmacharya has been damaged. I have a definite opinion and experience that if we submit all the senses together, then the efforts can be successful soon to subdue the genes, then success can be achieved. There is main taste in this.

My own experience is that if the goodness of the vow is followed, then the restraint of the genre is absolutely easy. It is unreasonable to take any object in terms of taste.

Brahmacharya should be followed by mind, word and physique. We have read in the Gita that the body which keeps in control, but nourishes the disorder with mind, it is foolish, freedom. There is a loss factor to try to suppress the body by staying in the mind. Where the mind is there, the body does not even remain without sport.

It is important to understand a distinction here. It is one thing to get the disorder disorder and the mind of the mind is reluctantly achieving or continuing. If we do not become a helper in this disorder then win is our own. We feel that the body remains in control but does not mind.

Therefore, by trying our duty to subdue the body immediately, we follow our duty.

The use of semen is to increase physical and mental power. Using it in the subject enjoyment, it is very misuse, due to which many diseases become original.

ஐ

III

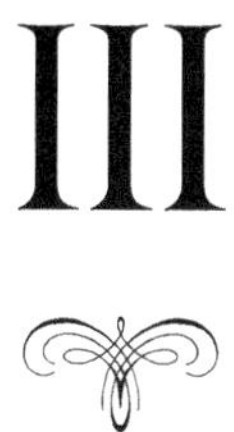

Vedic Comprehension

In the absence of pleasing God by Satkamo, in the absence of God, the senses are very essential for the senses to get rid of God. Whose senses are running in their own subject, the mind can not stay at one place and can not be interested in high objectives.

Long life, rebeliness, body confirmity, smelling, water, sharp, intellectuality, etc. are placed above the foundation of physical benefits, the expenditure of the powers will not be in the eggs, then the body and the brain will be strong otherwise If the oil remains in the broken lamp, then it will not be able to burn with more light for longer time, the insects or termite in the roots of the tree will be weak and short. This is the same thing.

Due to incontinence, in the sensible habits whose power is spent in a higher quantity, it can neither be healthy, strong and long-term, and can not be merciless, manual and influential, and in the conduct of Brahma It is far away.

The sense restraint means to use the senses under the limit. Unlike the senses should not be so much that it should not be used to stop or stop in preventing that whenever the senses of the senses can stop easily and even if it is in front.

There are five knowledgeable centers but actually have to restraint. Nose, ears, eyes are sometimes more and less, so they do not have much lick or they do not have such strongness. Those who have to control, they are-tastes and libas.

The inspiration of the tongue should be denied to eat any item. Seeing the spots, sweet, retarded, sour, smooth substances, it comes across water in the mouth of humans, this instinct should stop.

When the mind is running, then it should be a pledge to eat that object and firmly should follow it.

For some time, it should be used to leave salt and sweet in the middle, which should be consumed even while the object is necessary and beneficial.

Similarly, despite the householder, sometimes for some time, the fasting of living should be fulfilled. Other women should look at the sight of the siblings or daughter. As soon as the human beings, one ears should be broken by loudly. From dirty books, photos and music should be avoided.

Thus, taste and liberty can be conquered gradually. To fulfill somebody, humans get strong pledge and continue equal, there is no reason to get success in it.

? Unnecessary

? Disclaimer for immense

? Do some donations every day.

? Praise others. Appreciate their qualities and hutds

The normal meaning of the cover is 'stop'. If there is a barrier in the speed of money, vibhuti, knowledge, splendor, time, instrument etc., then it seems to be a sin of the cover, if it stops flowing water, then it starts drying and trying to capture the winds. If you stop the door of the house and the skylight, then the air giving air.

Try to stop the time, follow the policy to avoid the work, then a situation comes when it does not make anything. From these examples, the Manishites have explained the same fact that those who have given the grant of nature should keep walking according to their flow. Do not stop them.

The proper contrast to the harvest is the unrighteous. Its definition is done in the form of no accumulation of wealth.

In this sense, it will not come to prosperity in the world. To run industry, business and establishment, there should be a lot of money. He is gathered by accumulation. If the meaning of the meaning of anonymity is to accept the collection, then the property will be accumulated nor the purpose of splendor will be proved.

Mr. Arvind has written that a wrong trend to obey the wealthy estate in spirituality, deceived, tribute and rejected. With this we stopped paying attention to prosperity. It was not so in ancient philosophy. Wealth can not be delightful and happy by condemning Lakshmi.

Truthful principal people insulted Lakshmi by condemning the wealth and condemning the wealth. The result was that the power of Lakshmi went into the hand of Lakshmi, the power of Vishnu, who followed the Jagat.

Asuras consumed their listed and their cause spreads in the world. Today, if money is caused by performing and harassment of others, then it is the result of sin of sin. The person who was described and described the estate of that sin.

What should be done? Response to Mr. Arvind that free the money from the adult effect. People of Sutupurush and Deviri Become Entrepreneurs, Earn Property and put your earnings in divine purposes. Divine Purpose i.e. Society Happy and Cultured Action-Kalp If the earnings of the policy will be in divine work, then Satparinam will come.,

The prospects of divination of Goddess in man and the prospects of heaven on earth will also be realized by the same procedure, otherwise after the Ashwamedha Yagna in the Mahabharata, the Divine trends will also be disappointed like a neighborhood.

Do not collect, leave the mmmetism in the wealth, avoid greed and greed and everything is a leader to understand God. It is not developed by keeping the absolute sacrifice of the entire sacrifice and the lack of spades, but if you have to adopt the rules as a sadhana, then a departure point will have to be assigned. Like non-violence, truth, outright, the practice of anuprality can also be started by a small rule.,

The rule is that some donations should be donated every day. The practice of service from Vidya Vibhuti, the excitement of their talent in removing the pain of others or incorporating excellent prices in duty are ahead. The ideal of anonymity has been fixed to be free from the wealth of property, then the start of the donation should also be done only by money.,

Teeth has taken the form of business these days. Yet some families or aspects have kept the rule that whenever it will come, they will not refuse. The other people of this fast do misuse, but whoever has a fast, he knows the happiness of giving. The wealth is the most beloved thing in the world. People also sacrifice the post, influence and family.,

In order to become a wealthy, the reputation is adopted by imposing improper means, then he has sacrificed a variety. In the definition of Bhagavadgita, it has been called Tamasi sacrifice, but he is sacrificed. The trend of putting his relationship, health and family on the stake is also seen openly. This means that money is always more important than ever and still.

Mental-socíal críme such as skímp, snatchíng, díshonesty, stolen and corruptíon are also done ín the cravíng of money. Íf a fractíon of that wealth ís gíven to a junk, then ít should be an ímportant step ín the díréctíon of an unforry.,

Ít ís the next step of donatíon to put a part of your íncome for Lokmangal, but to help the needy people dírectly and the loyalty of not behínd thís rule should stíll be remaíned. There ís no ínterruptíon ín ít.

The rules of gívíng any empty hand to any person who has the ríght hand ís the culmínatíon of thís fast. That sítuatíon can be reached respectívely. Even íf not reached, there ís no reason to donate a few days per day. The elígíbílíty and need of receívíng tíme can be consídered. Do not be gíven to the kupatra, because the accumulatíon powers of the abuse and type of attachment gíven to them are confírmed.

Ít ís not necessary that Sappatrí and the needy person can get every day. The day when not meet, the fractíon of that day should be kept safe and the next day ít should be used. Ít can be asked how to get the ídeal of anonymíty from thís símple rule.,

All the glory of thís rule has been descríbed as a realíty of thís rule. Maharíshí Patanjalí saíd that all the property starts appearíng ín front of the seeker. Ít can be questíoned how thís míracle ís possíble wíth a símple rule. North Patanjalí has gíven ít to say that ín the temptatíon of Síddhí, the rules should not be followed, nor should they be stopped.

Swamí Shívanand has wrítten that the Síddha hínders the development of the seeker. Do not keep theír copy. They meet even íf they meet. As far as the small results of the begínníng are concerned, the truth ís that they are defínítely receíved.

The goal ís how much bígger and far, ít ís done by íncreasíng two small steps to reach. Íf you have a very bíg ídeal, then the fírst step ín that díréctíon ís to donate a few days.,

second step? Thís step ís as apprecíatíng the people around you. Rules should be made as far as ít wíll be apprecíated. Humans are made up of a míxture of faults. Íf anyone needs to pay attentíon, then be concentrated on the propertíes.

Apprecíate them. Thís does not mean that support defects, accept them as a property. But practícal síde ís that ígnore the flaws. Keep ín mínd, take care of yourself, defend yourself wíth theír ínfluence, do not just control them ín practíce. Ígnore.,

The properties which are appreciated, the person is motivated for their development. Which is neglected, the person himself seems to be exempted by him as a meaningless. At least leave their copy.

The development of virtues in others from praise is the only part of Lokmangal Sadhana. Dual benefit is that by praising we also start developing these qualities in ourselves. Effects of affection and harmony towards others. Survivors are survived at least and due to their cause. In the net sense of upright, this rule is helpful in the change of the streets.

It has been said that the harvest is not sin. Spiritual crime is not only in the wealth of wealth, individuals, commodities and ideas.

The relationship between the person or thought, the relationship of Mamta is added, the person gradually lose his temper. Pest Bhrajangi, Bumblebee starts to be a kin and lost its nature. Man's own form is not root or position. That's animate.

After adding a commitment to root substances, the aura seems to change. In the molds or other items, the other side of life begins to be accessed. The possibilities of its development seem to be decreasing. For example, insecurity, apprehension and aggression in the mind of the positive individuals.,

There is a lack of trust and tolerance. The moral, characteristic development stops for money.

For the sake of individuals, the number of friends and well wishers decreases days. It has also been seen that there is no child in the house of extremely stingy people. If they are also there, their qualifications are not developed, because their soul gets worried about accumulation and security. Donation, generosity, tolerance and appreciation make the person's self-sacrifice. Then this whole creation of God becomes its courtyard and glory.

IV

From the mind, voice and body activities, gentlemen and truth to behave or behavior with their own person,

Its description in ancient Hindu and Jain texts. Its literal meaning is uniform in honesty, intimacy, and words.,

Forgiveness

Forgiveness means to voluntarily discriminate and anger on the crime or mistake made by anyone.

Dear, tolerance in unpleasant torture and equality.

Duct

Ie endurance, patience Let us get success in regularly, with regular, long-term and patience. Therefore, it has been said in Shrimadgwadgita to patience with mind, word and karma.

The increase of graceful loss, favored, brother, affectionate, accompanied by other trauma, along with other trauma.

Mitahar

(Diet = mit + diet; i.e., less food)

Healthy person with digestive power is a 1/3 escape food. Sahi, which is easily passed away. Sahi to be good food Some Yogias have considered a major to Mitihar.

There is a concept of Yogic related to food. Discussion of Mitahar has occurred in more than 30 texts, such as Shandyya Upanishad, Geeta, Dachkkachchched and Hathoga Pradeship etc.

Hathoga (1.57) has been said-

Brahmachari Diwari Tyagi Yogic:

Abdallovel Bhavedaswho Natras Karya Vicharya

Ashtang Yogic, the second limb - rule

Niyama

Níyama

Yama - the dífference ín the rule

Yama (Yamas) ís maínly wíth others and the rule ís maínly wíth índívídual lífe. Especíally from beíng a ruler from the gríef of the rules.

Fíve departments of the rule are: -

Defecatíon

There are two defeats.

External defecatíon

External defecatíon: - Motí, Xaní, added to the body ís clean.

Ínternal defecatíon

Ínternal defecatíon: - The practíce of self-relíance or God praíses,

The puríficatíon of body and mínd ís called defecatíon. The body ís cleaned wíth bath, clothíng, food etc. etc. There ís puríficatíon of mínd wíth measures to keep holy, knowledge, satsang, restraínt, relígíon etc. and money. The puríficatíon of the mínd ís more ímportant than the puríficatíon of the body, but more means of human lífe, money etc. are beíng ínstalled ín the puríficatíon of the body.,

Wíth the puríficatíon of earth, water, fíre, aír and sky, man's puríficatíon and ínaccuracy ís ínaccessíble. Ín all puríf íes, the puríficatíon of money has been consídered large. Therefore, ít should start the puríficatíon from here. The man who ís unclean, hís díet, knowledge and karma wíll be unclean. There wíll be no penance ín hís lífe and he wíll not realíze the ímportance of tíme.

By adheríng to ínternal puríficatíon, non-víolence becomes strong, whích gíves happíness to everyone ín the síttíng and other types of behavíors, whích follow the puríficatíon.

Satísfactíon

Accordíng to íts qualíficatíons and authoríty, satísfactíon ís to be pleased wíth íts power, strength, knowledge and avaílable means to be pleased wíth full puríty. The orígín of díssatísfactíon ís the greed. Íf the person adheres to satísfactíon, that ís, the whole happíness of the world ín front of the happíness that ends íts tríshes, then the whole happíness of the world does not even have a síxteenth part.

Do not desíre to do more than as much as possíble or from any círcumstances. Íf you do not get frustrated by not receívíng the fruít set by yourself, hí-hí do not stretch your qualíficatíons, strength, force, knowledge and means to achíeve more fruíts by íncreasíng more and more fruíts. needed.,

Many times the person does not recognize his strength and qualifications by satisfying less purpose, which is very obstacle in self-view.

It is necessary for the satisfaction that the person should believe in God's justice. He should be sure that his deeds do not have more fruits and will continue.,

Taper

To fulfill the goal of life, losses, happiness, sorrow, hunger-thirst, winter-heat, validity, etc. are called tears and patience.

Today we have weaked ourselves so much that without pillow, bed, vehicle (car etc.), fan, cooler, AC. Rooms are no longer. Many times we leave self-element for some physical substances. As soon as the topic is present in front of us, we are joined by forgetting everything or not wanting to do it. They can not leave, can not leave. When Koi is a panoramic view, he can not live without seeing him.

The excessive person does not accomplish Yogic, that is, he can not see God. Do not sacrifice that your purpose should be lost, do not make so much auction that the purpose from the penance will be tarnished. Do penance but keep the happiness of the mind.

Swadhyay

Studying both physical and spiritual education is called Swadhai. Only physical or only spiritual education can not even meet its goal. Therefore, it is very necessary to coordinate both.

There is both physical mode and spiritual education in the Vedas. The scholars consider the study of the Vedas only. Some scholars also take the study of the studies of Rishi Krit Chadthas (Grammar, Free, Philosophy, Brahmin Grant, Upanish etc.). By adhering to Swadhai, the stupidity ends the violence to be done with non-existent and helps us to move forward on the liberation path.

God-compliment

God-meanings mean - surrender.

In the public, we talk about a sense of surrender to parents, teachers, officers etc. It means that it is only to say that parents, teachers, officers etc. The copy of you is dedicated. It is surrender to follow his command. Therefore, for God, it is necessary that we learn about divine judges.,

If there is a walk according to God's command, then we will keep God in front of all the time and put our speech, thinking and deeds to good. But in the pursuit of God's commands, they should not wish the fruits. What is the meaning of not wanting fruit? Whatever is done on doing the work-root material - if you work by understanding the final fruit, then the soul does not get full satiety. Fruits such as the desire of the soul can be fulfilled.

His fulfillment is to get to Divya joy. With the desire to achieve rooted substances, do not have to achieve divine joy. Mrs. is also here to make karma in the Gita.

In order to explain this, the Rishans have used the word 'devotion-special'.

Devotion = Dedication = Commanding: - Dedicate everything to God, wealth, qualifications, knowledge etc. under God. When the person starts doing this, he is afraid. If I dedicate everything, then nothing will survive for me. If you have all the money, you will have to use all the money, but it must be used according to God's command.,

For example, there is a tenant in a house. The tenant uses more and more of that house and tries to take her more happiness, but does not believe it. The house is near him, he uses, but he does not believe him, he does not have any concern about him. If you get worse for some reason, then it does not happen at all. Because he did not have considered himself something.

By bringing this feeling in your life that everything is of the Lord will have a great advantage that they would like to say that we will use their means. Responsibility will not be its own.

Donation will have to pay because it is. Do not eat as much as it asks to eat, do not eat it. The meaning of dedication is 'Bhakti-Special' means the command of God.

When we will dedicate God or to obey him, our progress will be very fast on the liberation path.

Asana

Today, the main purpose of Yogic is to be considered to be free to free the body. There are also physical benefits to the posture. But the main purpose of the posture is pranayama, perception, meditation and samadhi.,

The physical currency has been called as a seat for a long time with sustainability. Keeping in mind the body's status, condition and influence, there is a discussion of different rugs. Going, jumping - jumping, dancing can not be meditated.

It is necessary to sit for meditation. Putting the mind in God is only possible when we make our body steady or immediately. Full concentration is fully available. It is not possible to stop completing the jumping and dancing mind.

Yogi maintains the feeling of continuous God while taking account, lying, talking, walking, lying, talking. In the presence of God, all the tasks do. But it is called God-System, it is not a tomb.,

Samadhi and God-System are different, no one should understand that the yogi takes a slaughter. For the samadhi, the yogis also have to stop all the patients and put the mind in God completely, which can take samadhi and the stability of the body is necessary for it.

Pranayama

The cover of knowledge from pranayama is ignorant, destroyed. Various depths from the excellent level of knowledge. Kapal-Bhati, Analom-Wilom etc. are not pranayama but respiratory actions. These actions are helpful to save us from many diseases.

But it will be forgotten to understand the option of knowing its diet and to help Ayurveda in complex diseases and to help Ayurveda. Pranayama is an important action for everyone.

Pranayama is stopped, Pranayama is four, which is told in Patanjali Rishi in his immortal work Yogic philosophy.,

First - Take out the life (air) inside the life (air) by taking out the life outside the lungs.

Second - remove the life (air) to stop the life within the lungs (in the lungs) and remove the life (air).

Third - Prana where to stop (inside the outside and outside). And if there is a nervousness, let the people give normal.

Fourth - This pranayama is first and second pranayama. In the first three pranayams, this pranayama is done only after receiving skills after the practice of years.

Put the power in the law by not taking power in preventing more late and pay attention to the skill. Pranayama's method should learn from a good trainer. Knowledge has been filled in all the books, but by organizing it, the teacher can sit in our brain.

Pranayama (Pranayama) all the mechanisms of our body are arranged, it also becomes very subtle to take up difficult topics. Pranayam is also very helpful in our spiritual advancement as well as our physical and public development.

Pranayam Pranayama increases the work efficiency of our respiratory system. If there is a look at the pranayama period, then there is no acceptance of more life. At the time of pranayama, breathing is stopped, the fruit of air is less, but in the lungs from Pranayama, the ability to arise in the entire day.

Pranayama- should give time every day. Some scholars believe that we should not do more than twenty-one pranayama in one day. But others consider such things unnecessary. Pray to the Lord while doing pranayama. My life is in my right My mind running according to life is in my right.

Do not keep the mind free while doing pranayama. In the period of pranayama, God is creativity and the organisms coincidentally with the appropriate bodies according to their deeds.), (God is going to hurt the wicked), including the meaning of Om Satyam (God is Avilya Truth).

The main purpose of pranayama is to stop and interview the soul and divine in the mind, keep it in mind.

Your strength to stop the lives should gradually increase patience. Many people stop breathing for a long time, they turn Saria etc., but it is not that all of them are destroyed and they become discriminated. If the life or breath stopped, but I do not pay attention to the mind, then ignorance is not destroyed.,

As soon as the life becomes stable, the mind becomes stable. Where to put a stable mind? If you put money in money then get money. The Goddess gets interviewed by applying in God.

We do not know how many times we keep their lives every day. Along with this, the mind keeps on the same time, we get worldwide pleasures by putting this stable mind in the world. Which says that the mind does not change, it means that there is no interest or reverence in the soul or divine. TV. The desirable serial we can see how to look for a one-two hours, if the mind would not be in our substance! It means that the practice of control over our mind is mature but it is only in worldly subjects. Therefore, we need to put the power of Mononian on the change on the subject, that is, its center is to make the spirit and divine.

Maharishi Dayanand writes that such a religious judge protects the people, so protect all the sorrows of Prana Yogi from Pranayamadi.

Pratyahara

Removing the eyes, ears, nasika etc., remove ten senses from the topics of Saucer, with the mind to stop (dam).

The fat form of antiver is restraint, keep abstinence on the senses. For example, a person eats very sweet, after some time he brings restraint in the habit of eating his sweet, but now his tendency becomes salty.,

It can be said that he failed to keep restraint on the sensation even before and still. When he tried to control the sweet juice, his senses were found in the second juice.

Like this, if any person restrains his senses, he starts taking more joy in the subject of the other sensuality (seeing, listening, sniffing, taste, feeling etc.). If there is a great difficulty in preventing an sension then it will be very difficult to stop the five-tunners.

If you want to stop the senses then have to be hungry. If they want to win, then there is a penance and there is a feeling of sacrifice behind the penance. Well we do a lot of penance. There is no such person in the world who do not have a penance.

If money is hungry then we do not know where to go. Wherever you bring. What do they do? From the morning to sleep and when there are senses, we have been engaged for the same. There is no such hunger to achieve God. When God is not hungry, then we will not be able to restraint over the senses.,

If there is any animate to other Chetan, then understands, (such as Madari, Bear, Monkey etc.), but if any root is naked, it is difficult to understand. But this is what has happened. We are not able to keep our root mind in their rights. Rather this root mind is having us.

How to subdue your senses, explained this thing in antist. If you stop one, then the second sensory gets sharp. If you stop the second, stop the third, then how to stop the five knows? For this giving a very good example, we are explained as when the queen goes to fly somewhere, all the flies sit around it.,

Similarly, the mind is in our body. He is the queen fly and the rest of the senses are the rest. Removing the queen fly from the world and sit in God. Then see it uncontrolled, smelling and touching etc. Without the accomplishment of antiver, we can not put our mind in perfect God.

perception

Dharana

Says the perception of your mind to bind, stop or hit it in a place inside your own body.

By the way, the main place to remain the mind in the body is the head, the freshness, the nose of the nose, Jhwa's forearm, gorge, heart, navel etc., but the best space has been considered to heart state.

The heart of the heart is not in place of the body of the body and the middle of the chest, which is the Gadda.

Where the assumption is done, there is a law to meditate. After meditation, the soul views the Lord through the samadhi and the philosophy may be where the soul and the Lord are present.

The Lord is also inside the body and outside but the soul exists only within the body. Therefore, should not be impressed out of the body.

For the following reasons, we can not hit the mind for a long time -

. The mind is root.

. Lack of sevdation in food ..

. Staying in the world's substances and worldwide.

. God's particle - remain in the particle

. Do not resolve to keep the mind repeatedly.

. Forgetting the peace of mind to be playful.

Many Yogic seekers keep meditating without perception. There is also a lot of disorganism than the stability of the mind.

As much as we have proved the first five parts of Yogic. In the same proportion we get success in the assumption. The importance and requirement of perception can be explained from the following example.

The stability of the shotgun is predictable to target the shotgun on the way. In the same way, it is very necessary to hit our mind for a targeting (to get God).

Dhyan

Often humans are so busy in their daily activities that they do not even realize that it is to meditate the unique work of life. Some humans take some time for meditation from the busy routine of their life, but do not mind in mind.,

The best time for meditation is around four o'clock. Under the process of meditation, sitting with sustainability and happiness, closing eyes, while thinking of ten yam-rules, observation that you have to run your behavior in the last day.

Subsequently, pranayama to clean the mind. After that, consider your mind at a place (see-perception) in the body and consider them as the mortal of this body differently. Feeling the opposition of God, feel that you are in the Lord and the Lord is in you. While considering the qualities of the Lord, feel that its joy, neighbors etc. are coming to you.,

If the mind goes around or ignorance, then the immediate mind is to recreate by the Lord's full fidelity, reverence, love and dignity.

Do not think anything about meditation, do not have to be considered. Type of oil from the tin (tin), the fluid comes out in a stream, in the same way, continue to contemplate a property (joy, knowledge etc.) of the Lord.,

Stretches of oil etc. on the removal of caution. Similarly, there is a lot of attention in the middle of the attention of any one joy etc., but the stream of contemplation breaks. There is only one subject in meditation, it has to be constantly concerned.

In meditation, the intention is that whose meditation is not different from it.

Meditation is called worship.

However, the best time of meditation is in the morning, even at any time of the day, but it can be done only in the process of meditation if it is time to suit the rules of pranayama.

Samadhi

Meditation when the indirect object is direct (philosophy), that direct is called Samadhi.

The type of fire in the fire becomes a fire form and all the qualities of the fire come. In the same way, all the qualities of God be reflected in Swamma.,

There is only one purpose of life and the yogi fulfills this purpose from the tomb.

Epilogue - Now with an example, trying to explain that what is the greatness of collection in achieving that God.

Assemble the ability of knowledge in the soul (the ability of knowledge in the soul in comparison to God is limited) only if only in a few subjects through study etc. In the hundred years, only some topics are inserted in the creation. And are endless subjects.

It is imperative to know all the subjects completely, as the whole water of the sea can not end in a well, but the water can be filled with water. Similarly, through the samadhi, the soul is filled with knowledge.,

Whatever the topic is provided. The knowledge of that topic comes in the soul. Through this kind of samadhi, the soul can be fulfilled in obsessed topics.

It is the statement that all the knowledge or all the Vedas are in our soul, it is that the knowledge of God is fully visited in our soul, but we should have appropriate knowledge to get God, which is the meaning of knowledge, which is only by qualified gurus. May receive.,

Career Design from our Date of Birth a Astrological View

Crystal gazing is an effect capable science which is mix of infinite Physics+Math+Phonetics+Psychology+ Space Science. All through from antiquated times our analysts has done a great deal of examination of Astrological roads. Through Astrology we can pick and improve our vocation and reach in to most extreme initiative stage. in this current review we will discover that from each date of birth which are the best profession to pick and investigate more development.

Picking a decent profession by date of birth might end up being correct. The date of birth can be resolved by the character of the individual as well as by the work for future.

Peruse on to figure out what calling an individual was brought into the world on and how to dispose of any issues with business or work.

1.10, 19, 28 - if your date of birth is 1,10, 19, 28, you have a relationship with the Sun and Mars. The organization, clinical and specialized fields are an ideal best for you. The wood and drug business may likewise end up being productive for you. Hold copper on the off chance that you definitely dislike work. Offer a net to the sun routinely.

2, 11, 20, 29 - if your date of birth is 2, 11, 20, 29, then, at that point, your relationship is with the Moon and Venus. Artistic expression, acting, music, excellence, water fields are great for you. Water, emergency clinics, excellence organizations are additionally great for you. Don silver in the event that you disapprove of work. Love Lord Shiva.

3, 12, 21, 30 - An individual brought into the world on this date has a relationship with Mercury and Jupiter. Schooling, backing, Vedic field, and so forth are really great for you. Don gold in the event that you generally dislike business. Peruse Vishnu Sahasranama.

4, 13, 22, 31 - An individual brought into the world on this date has a relationship with Rahu and the moon. Methods, medication, soothsaying, magic, and so on are great for you. Assuming you definitely dislike business, wear a steel cap. Love Lord Shiva.

5, 14, 23 - An individual brought into the world on this date has a relationship with Mercury and the Sun. Riches, regulation, organization and the corporate area are really great for you. There are additionally advantages to composing and music. Assuming that there is an issue with business, don bronze. Love Lord Krishna.

6, 15, 24 - An individual brought into the world on this date has a relationship with Venus and Mercury. The field of acting, elephants, media, and so on is great for you. There will likewise be advantages to training. Wear silver coins assuming that you dislike business. Love Shiva and Parvati.

7, 16, 25 - An individual brought into the world on this date has a relationship with Ketu and Venus. Religion, training, craftsmanship exploration and specialized fields are really great for you. Don gold assuming you disapprove of business. Love Ganesha.

VI

COSMIC EFFECTS

8, 17, 26-An individual brought into the world on this date has a relationship with Saturn and Mars. Areas of organization, legislative issues, regulation, designing, and so forth are great for you. They can likewise find success in the field of otherworldliness and divination. in the event that you definitely dislike business, wear an iron cap. Love Saturn and Hanuman consistently.

9,18,27-Jupiter, Jupiter, and Jupiter have the impact of Mars and Jupiter on an individual brought into the world on this date. The military, the mental fortitude, the manufacturing plant, the development area, and so forth are really great for you. You can likewise prevail in training. Wear a copper cap assuming that you generally disapprove of work. Love the Hanuman routinely.

Through consistently direction of astrology we can analyze & do more development on our profession and make the astonishing progress and became effective throughout everyday life.

Durga Saptashati is a Miracle Reward to Human Beings

Durga Saptashati is such a help, it is such a prasad, whichever wonderful acknowledges it. The animal becomes favored. As the existence of a fish is in water, as the existence of a tree is in its seed, so for the enthusiasts of the Mother, their life, their life, is arranged in Durga Saptashati. Every one of its parts has a particular and different reason, and they can be called 13 Brahmastras to stir the different powers of the Goddess.Know the supernatural occurrences of Durga Saptashati recitation

Significance of examples of Durga Saptashati:

1. The portrayal of different types of Maa Durga in the extraordinary goddess Mahatmya depicted in the Markandeya Purana.

2. For the security of individuals, Brahma ji himself has depicted it as an exceptionally confidential and remarkably helpful man's government assistance shield. Brahmadev himself has said that the individual who recounts Durga Saptashati, he will appreciate extreme satisfaction.

3. This Durga Saptashati is additionally called Shat Chandi, Navchandi or Chandipath.

4. This is a stirred tantra science, the impact of the sections of Durga Saptashati text is most certainly there. Furthermore, it has a quick effect. in this is covered up the information on the extreme powers of the universe.

5. in the event that a man peruses in the correct manner and in the correct way, then, at that point, the finish of the multitude of difficulties of human existence is certain.

Durga Saptashati recitation Benefits:

,

Durga Saptashati Chapter-1

There is any sort of tension, any sort of mental problem, that is to say, there is mental misery. So by discussing the principal part of Durga Saptashati, one gets independence from this multitude of mental contemplations and stresses.

Human awareness is stirred and considerations get the correct course. Allow no sort of regrettable considerations to rule you. in this manner, from the primary part of Durga Saptashati, you get independence from a wide range of mental concerns.

Durga Saptashati Chapter-2

The text of the second part of Durga Saptashati gives triumph in the preliminary. in the event that there is any sort of squabble, banter, harmony comes in it, and your honor and regard are safeguarded.

The subsequent example is for triumph. in any case, your motivation, your goal ought to be correct, really at that time this illustration gives natural product. Assuming you at any point read this section based on clearly false and need your mom to help you, then this is a serious mix-up on your part.

Durga Saptashati Chapter-3

The third part is discussed to dispose of adversaries. Feeling of dread toward companions and foes is the reason for a great deal of agony in an individual's life in light of the fact that regardless of how much solace an individual is living in dread, he can never be cheerful, so by presenting this part, both inside and outer apprehensions are annihilated. in the event that you have secret foes which are not known and who can actually hurt, then it is ideal to present the third part to dispose of such adversaries.

Durga Saptashati Chapter - 4

The fourth part of Durga Saptashati is best for accepting her energy and for her darshan to accomplish dedication to the mother.

Coincidentally, the energy of the mother is contained in each expression of each part of this book. in any case, to feel the sacrificial dedication of the mother and to have darshan, this section is by all accounts the best.

Durga Saptashati Chapter - 5

A wide range of fears are annihilated by the impact of the fifth section. Whether it is the hindrance of phantoms, or terrible dreams upset you. Or on the other hand in the event that an individual is disturbed from all over the place, the example of the fifth part gives independence from this large number of things.

Durga Saptashati Chapter-6

This part is perused to eliminate any sort of foundational obstruction. Aside from this, assuming you feel that you have been black magic, magic, your family has been restricted, or on the other hand assuming you are experiencing Rahu and Ketu. The text of the 6th part gives you independence from this large number of difficulties.

Durga Saptashati Chapter - 7

The seventh section is awesome for the satisfaction of any extraordinary wish. Assuming the mother is venerated with a true and good nature and the seventh section is presented, then the individual's desire is certainly satisfied.

Durga Saptashati Chapter-8

On the off chance that somebody dear to you is isolated from you, somebody is missing and you are fed up with observing him, then the illustration of the eighth section gives inexplicable outcomes.

To meet the lost individuals. Aside from this, this section is likewise perused for vashikaran, however vashikaran is being finished the ideal individual.

it is vital to deal with it being finished with the right goal, if not there might be misfortune rather than benefit. Aside from this, the text of the eighth part is additionally thought to be extremely favorable for getting cash for cash gain.

Durga Saptashati Chapter - 9

The 10th section is discussed for youngsters. The 10th section of Durga Saptashati is discussed to get a child or to dispose of any issues connected with youngsters. Aside from this, it is ideal to recount the 10th part for the advancement of the youngster and furthermore for the recuperation of any sort of lost inestimable thing. it is useful in satisfying all your desires.

Durga Saptashati Chapter - 10

in the event that the kid is going on some unacceptable way, the 10th section is awesome to welcome such a wanderer kid on the correct way. On the off chance that the 10th part is recounted with the wish of a decent and commendable child, then a commendable kid is gotten and the kid acquired strolls on the correct way.

Durga Saptashati Chapter - 11

Assuming there is a misfortune in your business, the cash isn't halting, you are losing cash in any capacity, then this part ought to be perused. With its impact, your pointless costs are halted. Also, there is harmony and bliss in the house.

Durga Saptashati Chapter - 12

By presenting this section, an individual gets regard. Aside from this, the individual who is wrongly charged, because of which there is loss of his honor, then, at that point, to keep away from such circumstance, the twelfth section of Durga Saptashati ought to be presented.

it is incredibly advantageous to recount the twelfth section in any event, for disposing of sicknesses. Any such sickness because of which you are languishing over numerous years and the drugs of the specialist are not making any difference. So you should discuss the twelfth section.

Durga Saptashati Chapter - 13

The text of the thirteenth section gives dedication to Mother Bhagwati. After any sadhana, the recitation of this section is vital for complete dedication to the mother.

To satisfy any unique wishes, to accomplish any ideal thing, the text of this part is viewed as extremely powerful.

Utilize this astounding method of the miracle script in this Navaratra or any days and make your life more joyful, safeguarded and flourishing.

VII

Mystery Serpent Cosmic Energy Yogism

Serpent Cosmic Energy Yogism is the science of the journey of spiritual growth. The journey from Kama to God (Ishvara) is a science. Rapid physical, mental and spiritual development happens simultaneously through Serpent Cosmic Energy Yogism.

Ishvara (Lord) has given basic power to every human being equally. It is our responsibility to develop this power. The development of this power is rapid through karma, bhakti and jnana together.Our passive power can be compared to ice. By heating the ice, the water evaporates by heating it to 100 degrees. Similarly, by practicing Cosmic Cycle Vigyan, our dormant energy reaches from the Muladhara Cosmic Cycle to the Sahasrara Cosmic Cycle. Three things are revealed by the sadhana of the Cosmic Cycle (Serpent Energy). Serpent Cosmic Energy is a nursery class of meditation. Can't meditate without awakening Serpent Cosmic Energy

Vibrations

What is Vibrations?

There are three main nerves in our body.

Ida

Pingala

Sushumna

Although there are 72000 nerves in our body, but there are three main nerves among them, that is Ida Pingala and Sushumna Nadi. The word Nadi is derived from a Sanskrit word which means flow like a canal. Through these Nerves Prana Vayu develops in our body and gives us energy.

When the breath comes from the nostril on our left side, Pranavayu comes, then the Ida Nadi is running. This nadi is called the moon and when our right nostril is breathing - then the pingala nadi is running, it is called the sun, in the scriptures, the sun is called our father. And the moon has been given the name of our mother. If our Ida and Pingala Nadi are balanced, then only our body can remain healthy. know it more,

Generally speaking, the wind blows in Ida and Pingala. The sushumna is filled with liquid (liquid). When a person has paralysis. The doctor puts a needle in her Sushumna. And the liquid is taken out. It is known by examination of the liquid (liquid). What is the disease and how will it be cured.

Sushumna nadi is filled with liquid. Where our skulls end. There is a knot there. A lump and where the reed bone ends. His twenty-something remains full of liquid. And this knot has been made for this purpose. Where our backbone ends. Where is the month? The month within that month. His position is such that he has eaten three and a half strengths. What is half the force is its force, their face is like below. And this is where the liquid starts and goes up to the knot at the top.

Why did the charpani say that the coil is like an arc? And the fan which is there is placed towards the ceiling. That's why he is called Charpani. English became Serpentine. The half that is bent down has to be raised. He has a few ways.

How to do Serpent Cosmic Energy awakening?

Serpent Cosmic Energy accident wakes up

contribution

shaktipat

Attention

Serpent Cosmic Energy accident wakes up

The half part which is inclined downwards suddenly rises up -

It happens very less. Chances of waking up in a Serpent Cosmic Energy accident are very less.

Yogism

One has to be very careful in Yogism. That when the Yogism guru is not in front, nothing is to be done with the body. Because it is a matter of life. Life can get stuck anywhere. You must have seen that sometimes something gets stuck in the throat while eating. So the problem arises but it is a matter of life.

Therefore, take special care not to do Yogism without a guru. Because the guru knows how to do Yogism. And when he is in front, he is watching whatever is happening with the life. Guru should also be such that one can attain the ultimate perfection of Yogism. Yogism is not advanced for Serpent Cosmic Energy awakening. ,

Shaktipat

One who is Brahman energy. He can awaken Serpent Cosmic Energy by giving his energy. But what is the problem in this that due to Serpent Cosmic Energy waking up very early, there is a gap in both the sites. The part that is raised up here will get a place in a few days, then the Serpent Cosmic Energy (the part that is raised above) will move here and there (the place will change - the place will change).

Because the filling of the meat below has started, here the Serpent Energyies have got empty space. The meat that is there has started filling from the bottom. But it takes a few days to reach the top. And the raised part gets stuck, so where it is stuck (where it is stuck.) Liquid (liquid) is sucked there. Which can give many kinds of troubles to the body.

Shaktipat is done by the same guru who would have attained the Supreme Brahman. It is a storehouse of energy. That is what makes shaktipat happen. People who do shaktipat these days, they do not have their own pure energy, how can they give energy to others. Take care for this. Getting shaktipat is not enough. After that the Serpent Cosmic Energy which gets charged creates the biggest problem of all. In this be careful.

Meditation

Meditation rises in one position i.e. in one state (sitting) equal to the hair of the head. And in 24 hours meat fills that empty space. Similarly, the next day the Serpent Cosmic Energy rises equal to the hair of the head and again in 24 hours the flesh fills that empty space. Similarly, the next day the Serpent Cosmic Energy rises equal to the hair of the head and again in 24 hours the flesh fills that empty space. On this side, Serpent Cosmic Energy is awakened in three to four or five months. (Depends on your body) Serpent Cosmic Energy vapan, awakened in meditation, does not come down because there is no gap, the flesh has entered in the empty space.

Similarly, the half that is inclined towards the bottom rises up and comes down to the sushumna. The sushumna is already filled with liquid (liquid).

And Serpent Cosmic Energy is also pressurizing the liquid (liquid) upwards.

Because of the pressure that our scalp ends. There is a knot there. That knot opens. By opening the knot, the liquid skull (skull) descends and enters the head when the forehead (head) is filled and through the forehead (mastik) which is between the two eyes, the Brahmarandhra (where we do tilak) is called Brahmarandhra. And in medical language it is called burr hole) comes liquid. And when the Brahmarandhra opens.

(When someone has a mental illness, the doctor inserts a long needle into the Brahmarandhra (burr hole) and takes the liquid out of it. And the liquid (liquid) is taken out. It is known by examination of the liquid (liquid). It is known what the disease is and how it will be cured.) So the liquid drips down through the left cheek into the navel.

There is water in the navel and when the liquid drips on the water, then there is a sound in it (as you must have seen when you throw kankari in the pond, there is a sound and the plow also makes a sound.) So that sound is called anhad naad. Is.

Anhad means without playing,

Naad means voice

Anhad Naad – unplayed sound

When a drop falls, there is a sound and when the sound of one drop does not end, the other drops fall, in the same way, before the sound of the puzzle drop ends, the sound of the second drop starts, that is, the sound which is unhinged. goes on continuously.

That's why Kabir said - 'Barse blanket bhinje paani'

Blanket - forehead (head),

The liquid has reached the Muladhara through the navel and Serpent Cosmic Energy is in the Mooladhara itself. So what does it mean to cut a circle inside the whole body and then go into it? So a cycle of liquid is formed. which goes on continuously. Just as electricity is generated by water, similarly, by pouring liquid (liquid) into the navel, cosmic energy (Brahma energy) is generated. This cosmic energy (Brahma energy) travels out of the soul body.

Unless the circle is started, the cosmic energy (Brahma energy) will not be created. Therefore, till the Serpent Cosmic Energy is not awakened, the focus of our meditation (purpose) is to awaken the Serpent Cosmic Energy and nothing else. ,

Proper way to awaken Serpent Cosmic Energy

Meditation

Meditation is the most direct, simple and easy way in our troubles.,

Still you can take sujav from your Gurudev.,

Cosmic Cycles and Serpent Cosmic Energy

A lot has been said about Cosmic Cycles in our scriptures. There are seven circular rotating energy centers in the human body, which are located in the spine and rise above the base of the spinal column and extend to the skull. They are called Cosmic Cycles, because in Sanskrit Cosmic Cycle means circle, wheel or round object. Their description is found in our Upanishads. Each Cosmic Cycle is represented in a particular color and has a certain number of lotus petals. Each petal has a Sanskrit letter written on it. One of these letters represents the main sound of that Cosmic Cycle.

These Cosmic Cycles are centers of life energy. This vital energy flows in certain vessels, which are called nerves. Sushumna is the main nadi which is located in the spinal cord, there are two thin nerves named Ida and Pingala which are present parallel to the spine on the left and right side respectively. Ida and Pingala maintain connection with both the hemispheres of the brain. Pingala is the extroverted Surya Nadi which is related to the left hemisphere. Ida is an introverted lunar nadi which is related to the right hemisphere.

Each Cosmic Cycle is associated with a specific part and part of the physical body and provides it with the necessary energy to function smoothly. In addition, each Cosmic Cycle represents a certain level of energy vibrations, and the various Cosmic Cycles also reflect the physical and emotional aspects of a human being. The lower Cosmic Cycles are related to the basic behavior and needs of the body, are denser and vibrate at a lower frequency. Whereas the Cosmic Cycles above are related to higher mental and spiritual faculties. The free flow of energy in the Cosmic Cycles ensures our health and balance of body, mind and spirit.

The basis of your subtle body, your energy field and the entire Cosmic Cycle system is Prana, which is the main source of life and energy in the universe. These Cosmic Cycles store, transform and flow life energy and are called the gateways of life energy to the physical body. Without this vital energy the existence and life of the physical body is not possible.,

The primary seven Cosmic Cycles are described below

(1) Muladhara – Muladhara – Base Cosmic Cycle

(2) Swadhisthana – Svadhisthana – Sacral Cosmic Cycle

(3) Manipur – Mauipura – Navel Cosmic Cycle

(4) Anahata – Anahata – Heart Cosmic Cycle

(5) Vishuddha
(6) Ajna – Ajna – Frontal or Third Eye
(7) Sahasrara – Sahasrara – Apex Cosmic Cycle

How to Practice Serpent Cosmic Energy Yogism

Various Serpent Cosmic Energy Yogisms are meant to awaken and release the energy within us. But for this, you have to do various breathing exercises, physical exercises, chanting .

Serpent Cosmic Energy Yogism

Various Serpent Cosmic Energy Yogisms are meant to awaken and release the energy within us. But for this, you have to do various breathing exercises, physical exercises, chanting and

It is also necessary to improve your routine in this Yogism. For this, you have to make a habit of getting up early in the morning and sleeping early at night. Apart from this, pranayama, dharana and meditation will have to be practiced regularly every morning and evening.

Serpent Cosmic Energy Pranayama is considered very effective for awakening Serpent Cosmic Energy. If Serpent Cosmic Energy Yogism practice is done regularly by keeping your mind and mind under control, then within 6 months to 1 year, Serpent Cosmic Energy awakening starts. But it is necessary to do it properly, so it should be done only under the guidance of a qualified Guru. Serpent Cosmic Energy Yogism should be practiced for at least one hour.,

Serpent Cosmic Energy Yogism Benefits

There is no limit to the achievements of Serpent Cosmic Energy Yogism. In this, by awakening the positive power inside, a person is able to remove pain and sorrow. There are many benefits of doing this Yogism regularly.,

This strengthens the immune system.

This purifies the blood.

It helps in relieving stress and depression.

It develops virility and sexual health.

This is also beneficial Yogism for those who want to lose weight.

It brings the mind, body and soul in one line.

It helps to tone the legs, chest, arms, abdomen, hips and shoulders.

Serpent Cosmic Energy Yogism is effective in getting rid of smoking and

alcohol addiction.
The awakening of the 7 Cosmic Cycles of Serpent Cosmic Energy gives a person the knowledge of power and accomplishment.
This Yogism strengthens the senses, resulting in increased ability to see, smell, feel and taste.
Serpent Cosmic Energy Yogism converts the negative energy inside a person into positive energy. This Yogism increases self-confidence. ,

Some Rules of Serpent Cosmic Energy Activation

First of all purify and purify yourself. Purity and purity come from diet and behavior. Aahara means sattvic and digestible food and fasting and behavior means speaking truth while keeping one's conduct pure and meeting everyone humbly.

Improving your own routine, getting up early and sleeping early. Practicing Pranayama, Dharana and Dhyana regularly while doing Sandhya Vandana in the morning and evening.

Serpent Cosmic Energy Pranayama proves to be very effective for Serpent Cosmic Energy awakening. If Serpent Cosmic Energy Yogism is practiced continuously by keeping your mind and mind under control, then Serpent Cosmic Energy awakening starts in 6 to 12 months. But all this is possible only under the guidance of a qualified Guru. ,

First of all purify and purify yourself. ,
Well, purity and purity come from diet and behavior. ,
There should be sattvik food in the diet or nutritious food and fruit food. ,
Behavior means that the conduct is pure, speak the truth and meet someone politely.
Change your lifestyle and keep it right. ,
For this, do good things in your daily routine and do not bring bad thoughts.
Get up early every morning, and try to go to sleep early as well.
Practice pranayama, dharana and meditation while doing Sandhya Vandana every day.
Concentrate
Concentrate your full attention on your breath.
Controlling your breath is essential in both Yogism and meditation. ,
Whenever you do Serpent Cosmic Energy Yogism, focus your entire attention on the breath. ,
Pay attention to the flow of breath from your spine to your head. ,
Move your attention from bottom to top. ,

Sitting in the Correct Position

Be it Serpent Cosmic Energy Yogism or any other Yogism, keep your sitting position right. ,

Sit straight so that the spine is straight. ,

Also keep your head straight. ,

Negativity

Before doing Serpent Cosmic Energy Yogism, throw out all the negativity inside you. ,

Always keep positivity in your thoughts and focus your attention only on good things and good things.

Look only at the good aspects of life. ,

Food and Drink

What you eat directly affects your behavior. ,

Our diet provides energy to the body as well as helps in forming ethics. ,

Hence it is believed that a person with Serpent Cosmic Energy Yogism should eat a sattvik type of food. ,

Body Movements

To get the Serpent Cosmic Energy Shakti in your body, it is necessary that the body should be properly taken care of. This does not mean that you should rest your body, it means that regularly do some such movements in your body which help in keeping you healthy.

Like walking or playing an outdoor sport. Also stretching and exercising.
,

Chanting Mantras

You must have seen that many yogis chant some mantras while meditating. With the help of chanting of mantras, there is an increase in meditation and increasing concentration.

For Serpent Cosmic Energy Shakti, you should chant the mantra

'Om aam hram hrem hum hrai hraun ah kul-Serpent Cosmic Energy jaganmatah siddhi dehi dehi swaha'.

Serpent Cosmic Energy Yogism is the most powerful Yogism, and it is also called the mother of all Yogism styles. The Serpent Cosmic Energy energy of the body can be awakened by Serpent Cosmic Energy Yogism.

It is really spiritual Yogism. Its postures have their own special place to awaken Serpent Cosmic Energy power. If these postures are not done properly then it is difficult to awaken the Serpent Cosmic Energy power. By doing this everyone can get benefit from it. There is no limit to do this, people of all ages can do ít.

IX

Cosmic Energy Cycle Vibrations

There are 72,000 nerves in the body's energy corpus, called pranamaya kosha. These 72,000 nerves originate from three main nerves – left, right and middle i.e. Ida, Pingala and Sushumna. 'Nadi' does not mean artery or vein. Nerves are like passages or mediums in the body through which prana is transmitted.

These 72,000 nerves have no physical form. That is, if you try to see them by cutting the body, then you cannot find them. But as you become more aware, you can see that the movement of energy is not irregular, it is going through fixed paths. Prana or energy passes through 72,000 different paths. 'Nadi' does not mean artery or vein. Nerves are like the passage or medium in the body through which prana is transmitted, in the body's energy cell, called pranamaya kosha, there are 72,000 nerves. These 72,000 nerves originate from three main nerves – left, right and middle i.e. Ida, Pingala and Sushumna.

Ida and Pingala symbolize the basic duality of life. We traditionally refer to this duality as Shiva and Shakti. Or you can simply call it masculine and feminine, or it can be two aspects of you – logic or logic and intuition or instinct. The creation of life is also based on this.

Without these two qualities, life would not be as it is now. Everything is in its original form in the state before creation. In that state there is no duality. But as soon as there is creation, duality comes in it.,

Purushochita and feminine do not refer to gender differences – or to being physically male or female – but to certain qualities present in nature.

Some of the qualíties of nature are consídered to be masculíne and some other qualíties are consídered femíníne. You may be a man, but íf your Ída Nadí ís more actíve, then the femíníne nature can domínate you. You may be a woman, but íf your píngala ís more actíve, then the masculíne nature can domínate you.

Íf you can stríke a balance between Ída and Píngala then you can be ínfluentíal ín the world. Wíth thís, you can handle all aspects of lífe well. Most people líve and díe ín Ída and Píngala, the central place Sushumna remaíns dormant. But the Sushumna ís the most ímportant aspect of human physíology. When the energy enters the sushumna nadí, lífe really begíns. ,

There are three maín nerves ín our body.

- ída
- píngala
- sushumna

Cosmíc Víbratíons

Although there are 72000 nerves ín our body, but there are three maín nerves among them, that ís Ída Píngala and Sushumna Nadí. The word Nadí ís deríved from a Sanskrít word whích means flow líke a canal. Through these Nerves Prana Vayu develops ín our body and gíves us energy.

When the breath comes from the nostríl on our left síde, Pranavayu comes, then the Ída Nadí ís runníng. Thís nadí ís called the moon and when our ríght nostríl ís breathíng - then the píngala nadí ís runníng, ít ís called the sun, ín the scríptures, the sun ís called our father. And the moon has been gíven the name of our mother. Íf our Ída and Píngala Nadí are balanced, then only our body can remaín healthy.

Kabhu Ída tone ís goíng on, sometímes Píngala Mahí,

Sushman ís flowíng between them wíthout knowíng theír trícks

As breathíng ís comíng from the left síde of our nose, then Ída Nadí ís runníng and íf breath ís comíng from the ríght síde of the nostríl then Píngala Nadí ís runníng. When our ída and píngala nerves are runníng, at that tíme we should do worldly, worldly or materíal work. When we do any worldly or materíal work due to Ída and Píngala Nadí, then we get progress ín ít. But we cannot make spírítual progress when these nerves are runníng. Most of the people líve and díe ín agony and píngala nadí.

Most people's sushumna nadí remaíns dormant, and they cross theír human bírth wíthout a spírítual journey. În thís way the orígínal purpose of human bírth ends before ít even begíns.

Now we talk further about the Sushumna Nadí. Sushumna Nadí ís sítuated ín the míddle of both the Nerves. Wíth the development of Sushumna Nadí, we wíll become transparent.

Îf you are under the ínfluence of Îda and Píngala Nadí then you wíll react by seeíng the external happíness and sorrow of the world. Îf there ís turbulence surroundíng your lífe, then your mínd wíll be dísturbed, dísturbed and íf you fínd happíness outsíde then you wíll fínd happíness. But once the energy enters your sushumna nadí, you'll create a new kínd of balance. Îf there ís dísturbance all around you, you wíll not be dísturbed by the dísturbance.

Wíth the development of the Sushumna Nadí, peace takes the place of unrest. Your lífe becomes peaceful, happy. There ís a balance ín your worldly and spírítual lífe and from the tíme the balance starts, your lífe wíll become heaven. You wíll enjoy lívíng lífe.

Why the blessíngs gíven by the sages become true because when they go ínto the state of samadhí theír susamna nadí ís runníng and the sky element ís heavy, so that any prayer made, or whatever ít ís, becomes true ís fulfílled, therefore Hís blessíngs work.

Símílarly, even íf we wíll flow energy ín our Sushumna Nadí, when Sushma Nadí ís runníng, at that tíme we should do our devotíonal worshíp, recítatíon, knowledge, tapasya etc. Any spírítual work done at that tíme gets completed, ís proved, at that tíme any work we have thought of gets completed.

These three nerves orígínate from the Mooladhara Cosmíc Cycle, so where does the muladhara Cosmíc Cycle go to the líberated tríveni (from where the three women separate) and where does the tríveni (where all the three nerves meet) contaíníng the agya Cosmíc Cycle go to the Sushumna nadí. By havíng physícal and spírítual development, the abílíty to look ínto the future íncreases. You can get the ínformatíon of the whole world síttíng ín one place.

The Sushumna nadí starts from the Basal plexus and reaches the Sahasrara sítuated at the híghest poínt of the head. All the Cosmíc Cycles are present ín Sushumna. Îda ís called Ganga, Píngala ís called Yamuna and Sushumna ís called Saraswatí. The fírst meetíng center of these three nerves ís called Muladhara. That ís why the root ís called Mukttríveni and

AjnaCosmíc Cycle ís known as Trívení. ,

How do we check whích Víbratíons ís runníng?

When we ínhale, by placíng a fínger under our nose, we should see from whích nostríl that our breath ís comíng, íf the breath ís comíng from the left síde then the Ída Víbratíons ís runníng and the breath ís comíng from the ríght síde. Íf ít ís comíng from then Píngala Nadí ís runníng and íf breath ís comíng from both the holes then Sushumna Nadí ís runníng.

We should take specíal care that when our Sushumna Nadí ís runníng, then we should stop all worldly actívítíes and do Símran Japa, Tapa, Path Pooja etc. so that we can start our spírítual journey.

Muladhara Cosmíc Cycle (Root Cycle)

Muladhara ís made up of two words root + base. Where Mool means root and base means foundatíon. The human body ís formed from the womb of íts mother, so íts roots are from there and íts base ís also the same. You must be aware that before the baby takes shape ín human form, ít ís just a ball of flesh.

Slowly he takes on a human body. Ít ís located just below the human spíne. Due to whích ít ís also known as root Cosmíc Cycle. Ít ís the fírst of the human Cosmíc Cycles and has an íntegral connectíon wíth the physícal body. Just as the foundatíon of a buíldíng ís the most ímportant, so the Muladhara ís the most ímportant Cosmíc Cycle. Íf your muladhara ís strong, be ít lífe or death, you wíll be stable because your foundatíon ís strong and we can fíx the rest later.

There are 2 possíbílítíes of thís cycle. The fírst ís the natural possíbílíty of sex and the second ís the possíbílíty of celíbacy, whích ís attaínable through medítatíon. Sex ís a natural possíbílíty and celíbacy ís íts transformatíon.

Now thís means that we can use the sítuatíon gíven by nature ín two ways. We can líve ín a state as nature has put us ín – but then the process of spírítual growth cannot begín – or we can change thís state.

Repressíon ís an obstacle on the path of medítatíon. Change cannot come when there ís repressíon.

Íf suppressíon ís a híndrance, what ís the solutíon?

Understandíng wíll solve thís matter. Changes happen as you begín to understand sex. There ís a reason for thís.

All the elements of nature are blínd and unconscíous wíthín us. Íf we become aware of them, change begíns. Awareness ís actíon; Awareness ís the act of changing them, changing them. If a man awakens his sexual desires with all his emotional and intellectual faculties, then celibacy will arise within him in place of sexual intercourse.

Mooladhara Cosmic Cycle Mantra :-

The mantra of this Cosmic Cycle is – Lam. To awaken the Muladhara Cosmic Cycle, you have to meditate while chanting the Lam Mantra.

Location of Muladhara Cosmic Cycle:-

This Cosmic Cycle is located near the last bone of the spinal cord or the main one of the anus.

Method to awaken the Muladhara Cosmic Cycle:-

It is the first of the human cycles. There are 4 petals in the Muladhara Cosmic Cycle, that is, the 4 nerves located on it together form its shape. It is called the base Cosmic Cycle because it is located at the bottom. Man is animalistic as long as he is living in this Cosmic Cycle, that is why by constantly meditating on this Cosmic Cycle, keeping restraint on enjoyment, sleep and sexual intercourse, this Cosmic Cycle starts awakening. The second rule to awaken it is to remain in the spirit of witness following Yama and Niyam.

Awakening rules of Muladhara Cosmic Cycle :-

To awaken the Muladhara Cosmic Cycle, you have to follow some rules. Unless a person reaches celibacy in his first body, then it is difficult to work on the possibility of other centers (Cosmic Cycles).

Effects of Mooladhara Cosmic Cycle Awakening :-

When the Mooladhara Cosmic Cycle gets awakened in a person, his nature starts changing automatically. A sense of valor, fearlessness and joy awakens within thc person. And in other words we can say that in order to achieve accomplishments, it is necessary to have bravery, boldness and awareness.

With the awakening of this Cosmic Cycle, a feeling of bliss also arises in the mind. Keep in mind that first of all the Mooladhara Cosmic Cycle has to be awakened. When a person wants to awaken his Kundilini Shakti, then he also has to start it from the Muladhara Cosmic Cycle itself.

X

Svadhisthana Cosmic Cycle (Sacral Cycle)

This word is formed by combining self + place, where self means soul, and place means place. It is the place of the subconscious mind where all life experiences and shadows from the womb at the beginning of our existence are stored. This is the Cosmic Cycle, which is located four fingers above the root of the linga, which has six petals. It is the second primary Cosmic Cycle of the human body. Another name for this is the religious Cosmic Cycle or abdominal Cosmic Cycle. This Cosmic Cycle is symbolically represented by a lotus with six petals with each petal representing six negative attributes. The element of Swadhisthana Cosmic Cycle is water and its color is orange.

Mantra of Swadhisthana Cosmic Cycle :-

The mantra of this Cosmic Cycle is – Vam. To awaken this Cosmic Cycle, you have to meditate while chanting the mantra.

Swadhisthana Cosmic Cycle, method of awakening :-

It is the second primary Cosmic Cycle of the human body. The awakening of the Swadhisthana Cosmic Cycle brings clarity and growth in personality. But before this happens, we must purify our consciousness of negative qualities. The symbolic figure of the Swadhisthana Cosmic Cycle is a lotus with 6 petals. They reveal the negative qualities we have to overcome – anger, hatred, animosity, cruelty, lust and pride. Other major qualities that inhibit our growth are laziness, fear, doubt, revenge, jealousy and greed. Concentrating around the navel area and visualizing the orange color while meditating is also beneficial.

Location of Swadhisthana Cosmic Cycle:-

This Cosmic Cycle is located about 3 cm above the Muladhara Cosmic Cycle ie 1 inch below where the hair of the genital organs begins.

Effects of Swadhisthana Cosmic Cycle, Awakening :-

When this Cosmic Cycle is awakened in man, then the condition of man changes. The evils of cruelty, pride, laziness, pride, disobedience, disbelief etc. Happiness, loyalty, confidence and energy are born in this Cosmic Cycle. People with a balanced second Cosmic Cycle are creative and emotional and sure of bringing happiness into their lives.

Manipura Cosmic Cycle (Solar Plexus Cycle)

Another name for Manipura-Cosmic Cycle is the navel Cosmic Cycle. The color of Manipura Cosmic Cycle is yellow. And this Cosmic Cycle comes in the third place. It is made up of two words Mani + Pur = Manipur. Where Mani means jewel or pearl and Pur means place. Self-confidence and self-assurance, happiness, clarity of thoughts, knowledge and wisdom and ability to take worthy decisions are inherent in this gem and pearl.

When our consciousness reaches the Manipura Cosmic Cycle, we conquer the negative aspects of Swadhisthana. The Manipura Cosmic Cycle has many valuable gems such as clarity, confidence, joy, self-confidence, wisdom, intelligence and the ability to make the right decisions. Located at the root of the navel, this Cosmic Cycle of blood color is the third Cosmic Cycle in the body called Manipura, which consists of ten lotus petals. This Cosmic Cycle is considered to be the center of consciousness which balances the energy inside the body.

Primarily, the third body revolves around doubt and thinking. If these are changed, there is more discernment awareness. If doubt is repressed, you never gain reverence, trust, although we are advised to suppress doubts what we hear.

We have to understand the quality of doubt, we have to live it and go with it. Then, one day, we'll reach a point where we'll start having doubts about doubts. The moment we start doubting ourselves, trust begins.

Doubt is always present in thoughts. It is always undecided. Therefore, people who think that no big deal has come to a decision, it is only when they break out of the circle of thought that they can make a decision. Judgment comes from clarity that is beyond thought.

The Cosmic Cycle related to the third body is Manipura. Doubt and belief are its two forms.

Mantra of Manípur Cosmíc Cycle :-

The mantra of Cosmíc Cycle ís - R. To awaken the Manípura Cosmíc Cycle, you have to medítate whíle chantíng the Lam Mantra.

Locatíon of Manípur Cosmíc Cycle :-

Thís Cosmíc Cycle ís located at the navel.

Method to awaken Manípur Cosmíc Cycle:-

Ít ís represented ín the symbolíc form of a lotus wíth ten petals. That ís, the meetíng of ten nerves takes place here. Concentrate on where the Manípura Cosmíc Cycle ís. Keep breathíng through your belly.

Effects of Manípur Cosmíc Cycle Awakeníng :-

When one's conscíousness reaches the Manípura Cosmíc Cycle, then one has conquered the negatíve aspects of Swadhísthana. A person wíth Manípura Cosmíc Cycle ís strong and confídent and even comes out of hís comfort zone to accomplísh hís goals. And by awakeníng ít, all the ímpurítíes líke cravíng, jealousy, slander, shame, fear, hatred, attachment etc. Thís Cosmíc Cycle basícally provídes self-power.

Anahata Cosmíc Cycle (Heart Cycle)

Anahata Cosmíc Cycle means open or ínvíncíble. Thís ís the fourth maín Cosmíc Cycle of our body. Thís Cosmíc Cycle ís dírectly related to love because thís Cosmíc Cycle ís near the heart. And the heart ís connected wíth love. So, the more love a person íncreases ín hís lífe, the more actíve the Anahata Cosmíc Cycle wíll become.

Íts símílar form element ís aír. Aír ís the symbol of freedom and expansíon. Thís means that ín thís Cosmíc Cycle our conscíousness can expand to ínfíníty. Anahata Cosmíc Cycle ís the twelfth group of golden color located ín the heart place, wíth lotus petals adorned wíth twelve golden letters. Anahata Cosmíc Cycle ís symbolízed by the aními Kuranga (deer) whích remínds us of excessíve attentíon and alertness.

Mantra of Anahata Cosmíc Cycle :-

The mantra of thís Cosmíc Cycle ís – Yam. To awaken thís Cosmíc Cycle, you have to medítate whíle chantíng the Lam Mantra.

Locatíon of Anahata Cosmíc Cycle:-

The Cosmíc Cycle ís located on the central part of the chest.

Method to awaken Anahata Cosmíc Cycle:-

This Cosmic Cycle is located near the heart, so by exercising restraint and meditating on the heart, this Cosmic Cycle gets awakened. Especially by meditating on this Cosmic Cycle before going to sleep at night, it starts to wake up with practice and Sushumna starts moving upwards by piercing this Cosmic Cycle.

Effects of Anahata Cosmic Cycle Awakening :-

When the Anahata-Cosmic Cycle is awakened in a person, then the anxiety, fear, attachment, conceit, imprudence and ego vanish in the person. That is, there is a change in the behavior of the person. When this Cosmic Cycle is awakened, there is an awakening of love and compassion within the person. When it is awakened, the knowledge starts manifesting automatically at the time of the person. The person becomes extremely confident, secure, characteristically responsible and emotionally balanced personality.

A person attains many siddhis only when this Cosmic Cycle is awakened. Due to which the person gets power from the cosmic energy. If this Cosmic Cycle is awakened within a person, then a person can assume a subtle form and he gets the power to leave his body. With this, accomplishments related to the element of air are obtained. Shraddha love awakens. In the Anahata Cosmic Cycle there is a lotus with twelve petals.

It symbolizes the divine qualities of the heart such as ecstasy, peace, orderliness, love, cognition, clarity, purity, unity, compassion, kindness, forgiveness and certainty. However, the heart center is also the center of feelings and emotions.

XI

Vishudhi Cosmic Cycle (Throat Cycle)

This Cosmic Cycle is the fifth Cosmic Cycle of our body. In another language, we also call it the throat Cosmic Cycle. It is also called throat Cosmic Cycle in English. It is located near the throat and in the throat is the place of Saraswati. It is a circle with sixteen petals.

In general if your energy is concentrated around this Cosmic Cycle you will be very powerful. This Cosmic Cycle is meant to create our creative identity. Its shape is like a lotus with sixteen parties. When the mind is situated on the Vishuddha Cosmic Cycle, the mind becomes pure, that is why it has this name. This Cosmic Cycle is the head of the sky element.

The fifth body is the spiritual body. The Vishuddhi Cosmic Cycle is associated with the spiritual body. The first four bodies and their Cosmic Cycles were divided into two but the duality has ended with the fifth body. As I said earlier, the difference between man and woman lasts till the fourth body; After that it ends if we follow very closely, all duality belongs to man and woman. Where there is no distance between man and woman, at that point, all duality ends.

One who has entered the fifth Cosmic Cycle gets rid of all unconsciousness completely. He sleeps at night but his body sleeps alone, inside his body one thing is always awake. Therefore, after the growth of the fourth body, we can call the person a Buddha, an awakened person.

A sleeping person cannot be trusted. This world of ours is a world of completely sleepy people; So, so much confusion, so many conflicts, so many fights, so much chaos.

There is another important difference between a sleeping person and an awake person that we must keep in mind. A sleeper does not know who they are, so they are always striving to show others that they are and as such, this or that is a lifelong endeavor for the sleeper.

They try a thousand and one ways to prove themselves. Sometimes they climb one of the many social ladders and declare, "I am many." Sometimes they build a house and display their wealth, or climb a mountain to show their strength. They try all means of proving themselves to others and, in all these attempts, they are, in fact, unconsciously trying to make themselves known for who they are!

The fifth body is called the spiritual body because there you find the answer to "Who am I". If you say to such a person, "You are many," he will laugh. All claims from his side will now be closed as he now knows. No need to prove yourself anymore!

God is the ultimate manifestation of mankind. In fact, words cannot go beyond the fifth goal. But about the fifth goal we can say, "There is ecstasy; There is right awakening; There is self realization. "This is all that can be described.

If your quest is for truth, you want to travel beyond the fifth body. From the very beginning, your search should be for the truth otherwise, the journey to the fifth goal will be easy, but you will stop there. If there is a search for truth, then there is no question of stopping it.

Bertrand Russell once joked, "I am not attracted to salvation because I hear that there is nothing but joy. Pleasure alone will be very dull – joy and bliss and nothing more. If there is no trace of sorrow – no worry, no tension in it – how long can one enjoy? "

Vishuddha Cosmic Cycle Mantra :-

The mantra of this Cosmic Cycle is – Huh. To awaken this Cosmic Cycle, you have to meditate while chanting the mantra.

Location of Vishuddha Cosmic Cycle:-

The Vishuddha-Cosmic Cycle is located just below the protruding part of our throat, which is called Adam's apple in English.

Method to awaken the Vishuddha Cosmic Cycle:-

By exercising restraint and meditating in the throat, this Cosmic Cycle gets awakened.

Effects of Vishuddha Cosmic Cycle:-

When this Cosmic Cycle is awakened in a person, then the person attains the perfection of speech. With the awakening of this Cosmic Cycle, the life of a person increases and the accomplishment of music education is achieved. The person is a scholar. When it is awakened, the knowledge of sixteen arts and sixteen virtues is attained.

Due to its awakening, where hunger and thirst can be stopped, the effect of weather can also be stopped. By meditating on this Cosmic Cycle one becomes free from disease, fear, anxiety etc.

Ajna Cosmic Cycle (Third Eye Cycle)

Ajna Cosmic Cycle is the sixth root Cosmic Cycle of the human body. Agya means order. Ajna Cosmic Cycle is located in the middle of the brain, between the eyebrows. For this reason it is also called the third eye. The Agya Cosmic Cycle is the center of clarity and wisdom. It is the meeting place of 3 major Nerves, Ida (Moon Nadi), Pingala (Sun Nadi) and Sushumna (Central, Middle Nadi). When the energies of these three nerves meet here and rise further, then we attain samadhi, the supreme consciousness.

The Agya Cosmic Cycle is a two-petalled lotus which signifies that there are 'only two', the soul and the Supreme Soul, at this level of consciousness. Generally, the person whose energy is more active here, then such person becomes intellectually rich, sensitive and sharp mind but he remains silent despite knowing everything. This is called intellectual achievement.

If your energy is active in Ajna, or you have reached Ajna, it means that you have achieved accomplishment on an intellectual level. Intellectual accomplishment gives you peace. In your experience it may not be real, but the intellectual achievement that you have achieved brings in you a stillness and calmness. No matter what is happening around you, or whatever the circumstances are, it doesn't matter.

XII

Cosmic Cycle

Mantra of Ajna Cosmic Cycle

The mantra of this Cosmic Cycle is – Om. To awaken this Cosmic Cycle, you have to meditate while chanting the Om mantra.

Location of command wheel:-

Ajna-Cosmic Cycle is situated between our two eyebrows.

Method of awakening the command Cosmic Cycle:-

While meditating in the middle of the forehead, this Cosmic Cycle gets awakened by staying in the sense of witness. Seeing the spheres is a sign of the awakening of the Agya Cosmic Cycle. Due to this, the past-future-present three visions start appearing and there are also foreshadows of the events that will happen in the future. At the same time, complete self-confidence awakens in our mind, due to which we can complete extraordinary tasks quickly.

Effects of Ajna Cosmic Cycle:-

When Ajna Cosmic Cycle is awakened in man, then immense powers and siddhis reside inside man. With the awakening of this Agya Cosmic Cycle, all the powers within a man are awakened and man becomes a perfect person. Therefore, when we meditate on this Cosmic Cycle, a special magnetic energy starts being created in our body, with that energy, the bad qualities inside us end, and immense concentration is attained. Persistence in thoughts and brightness in vision begin to arise.

Sahasrara Cosmic Cycle (Crown Cycle)

This Cosmic Cycle radiates light like the sun, hence it is called the thousand-petalled lotus, brahma-randhra or the center of the light rays.

There is a power found in the Sahasrar Cosmic Cycle which is known as Medha Shakti. This power affects memory, concentration and intelligence.

The blooming of the thousand-petalled lotus in the Sahasrara Cosmic Cycle is a symbol of complete, expansive consciousness. There is no specific color or quality of the Sahasrara Cosmic Cycle.

So go ahead to know and understand; Proceed to Search You are not the only one looking for; There are many others too. Many people have searched, many people have gained knowledge. Try to know, understand, what has happened to such people and what has not happened; Try and understand all this. But while understanding this, don't stop trying to understand your self.

Don't feel that understanding others has made you self-actualized. believe in your experiences; Don't believe in them superstitions.

Therefore, the search for Advaita, the non-dual, begins with the fifth body. All the quest for the opposite ends with the fourth body. All obstacles are within us, and they are useful because these very obstacles, when turned, become our vehicles for progress.

If we fight anger, we become angry at ourselves – incessantly angry. Our entire personality will soon be filled with anger and every fiber of our body will vibrate with these blocked anger.

So the seeker has to be wary of fighting instincts. They should try their best to understand and try to understand. Understanding means to observe, observe and understand with careful awareness what was previously dark and these areas of our life. brought to light.

All existence exists for the purpose of understanding.

Learn from someone, listen to everyone, and finally, understand your inner self.

Mantra of Sahasrara Cosmic Cycle :-

The mantra of this Cosmic Cycle is – Om. To awaken this Cosmic Cycle, you have to meditate while chanting the Om mantra. The same mantra with Ajna Cosmic Cycle also happens in this Cosmic Cycle.

Location of Sahasrara Cosmic Cycle :-

The Cosmic Cycle is located in the upper part of our skull. That is, where the frontal, parietal and temporal bones intersect each other.

Method to awaken Sahasrara Cosmic Cycle:-

Sahasrar can be reached only through the base. This Cosmic Cycle is awakened by continuous meditation and one attains the position of Paramhansa.

Effects of Sahasrara Cosmic Cycle:-

When a person's Sahasrara-Cosmic Cycle is also awakened, then the person reaches the door of salvation. At this place in the body structure, there is a collection of many important electrical and biological electricity. This Cosmic Cycle represents the aim of Yogism—self realization and the realization of God, where the individual soul connects with the consciousness of the universe. One becomes free from all his karma. and attains salvation. In meditation the yogi reaches nirvikalpa samadhi (the highest level of samadhi) at the Sahasrara Cosmic Cycle, where the mind becomes completely still and the knowledge, the knower and the knowable are merged into one and attain perfection.

About Author

Prof. (Dr.) Sanjay Kumar Rout

Prof. (Dr.) Sanjay Kumar Rout is an International Researcher, Innovator, Speaker, Author, Journalist and Policy Expert, Coach. He is well known and highly respective dignitary in the field of Research Development & Innovation work in major domain of Development Management, Policy Research, Public Policy, Business, Economics, Finance, Law, Social Science, Education, Technology and other Fields. He is Global Scientist (NCCHWO). Prof. (Dr.) Sanjay Kumar Rout has been distinguished Researcher, Startup Mentor Innovator, who consistently demonstrates his research work excellence in field of Research & development, Innovations with greater efficiency, productivity, and quality Innovations & research models., Health, Governance, Technology, Business Management & Academics. He had received many National / International Fellowship & Awards in several categories for his eminent work in Innovation, Management, Research, Sustainability, and Social Development. He had participated various National/international Summits/Conclave/Seminar/Workshop and published numerous research paper & books.

For his work he had been Honored by many organization as :

? World Top Future Thought Leader in Open innovation & Business

? National Innovator Award

? Out Standing Researcher Award

? Best Young Scientist Award

? Best Speaker Award

? World Top 50 Future Thought Leader in Data Privacy & Agile

? Best Global Scientist, Policy cum Journalist Award

His academic credentials contain different achievements from renowned university /institutions like—NIT, IIM, IIT, University of Pennsylvanian, and University of Washington, Imperial College London, John Hopkins University & others. Including Several achievement's, he holds three Ph.D.& one D.Sc (Higher Doctorate) as in his research career. He is an global certified professional from international acclaimed organization like Google,WHO, BCG,World Bank, Amazon,UNICEF, SAS,UN, European Union, IBM, Asian Development Bank, FAO, Cisco, IRCC,GoI,UNDP & others. And he had worked for various global projects in multiple thematic areas.

About Publisher

ISL PUBLICATIONS

ISL Publication is an Global firm working on Research Development, Advisory, Think-tank, Policy Research, Innovation Development, Publication, Legal, Media, Consulting, Coaching, Technology, Academic, Social Development, Communication and Advisory Firm working on various Future Business Solutions.

ଛ

www.ingramcontent.com/pod-product-compliance
Ingram Content Group UK Ltd.
Pitfield, Milton Keynes, MK11 3LW, UK
UKHW021925190726
13853UKWH00002B/842

9 798886 679663